Established 1971
Arthur's Shoe Tree®
"Personalized Fitting Is OUR Speciality"

Arthur's Shoe Tree has been providing a specialized fitting service for over 36 years that is not available in most shoe stores. Our trained staff actually measure, evaluate, suggest, try on and fit your feet! Arthur's realizes and takes into consideration what a customer "wants", but tries to explain why certain shoes will work and why certain shoes won't work for a particular customer's problem. If you have orthotics (full or three-quarter), heel lifts, special AFO (Ankle/Foot Orthotic) braces, need special diabetic fitting or just have hurting feet then you need **Arthur's Shoe Tree** for the "FIT" of your life.

Arthur's is the store the doctors recommend, for all of your fitting problems. We carry name brand shoes in sizes and widths to fit every member of your family.

Ron Brandich on his first day of ownership of Arthur's, April 1971.

Ron Brandich and his store in 2007.

1144 CLEVELAND RD., SANDUSKY • 419-626-0463
IN THE SANDUSKY PLAZA
HOURS: Mon. thru Fri. 9:30-7:00; Sat. 9:30-6:00

CLOSED FOR LUNCH 1:30-2:30

Star Lanes
Three generations of family entertainment

A bowling dynasty began in Sandusky in 1963, when John and Rita Tintinalli, and Walter and Mable Miller opened their state-of-the-art facility. These beloved paternal and maternal sets of grandparents passed the love and art of bowling to their son, Bruno, and grandsons, John and Jeff. The bowling alley was built by Ed Feick and Hank Shenigo and proudly stands to this day. The business was purchased by Bruno Lizzi in 1991. In 2007, Lizzi transferred ownership to his sons, John and Jeff. Although the sport of bowling has transitioned throughout the years, it remains a high-profile sport and solid family entertainment.

2097 Cleveland Road • Sandusky • 419-626-2413

A Pictorial History 1940-1975

ERIE COUNTY
& THE ERIE ISLES

PRESENTED BY THE SANDUSKY REGISTER AND THE SANDUSKY LIBRARY

Acknowledgments

We wish to thank the hundreds of community members who came forward with historical photographs from family collections that made this book possible. The tireless efforts of Sandusky Library's Ron Davidson, archives librarian, and Maggie Marconi, museum curator, who helped select and organize the photographs, and Lori Schrader, public relations specialist, for administrative assistance, also enabled publication of this book. The library's board of directors, past and present, also deserves credit for maintaining policies since 1901 to collect and preserve important historical documents. Members of the Register newsroom staff, including Kathy Lilje, Charles "Butch" Wagner, Karen Mork and Cheryl Welch also contributed time and energy to this effort, and William "Bill" Ney, the Register's circulation director, gave countless hours guiding the publication and distribution of this book.

Copyright© 2007 • ISBN: 1-59725-111-9

All rights reserved. No part of this book may be reproduced, stored in a retrieval system or transmitted in any form or by any means, electronic, mechanical, photocopying, recording or otherwise, without prior written permission of the copyright owner or the publisher.
Published by Pediment Publishing, a division of The Pediment Group, Inc. www.pediment.com Printed in Canada

ERIE COUNTY & THE ERIE ISLES 1940-1975

TABLE OF CONTENTS

FOREWORD 4

PUBLIC SERVICE 5

CELEBRATIONS 24

DISASTERS 32

RELIGION 36

EDUCATION 42

SPORTS & LEISURE 62

THE LAKE & THE ISLES 74

COMMUNITY 81

COMMERCE 93

INDUSTRY 101

FAMILY & FRIENDS 111

VIEWS 121

FOREWORD

We were Americans first but cherished our roots and tended to stay within the neighborhoods, churches and social clubs our German, Italian, Irish or African-American ancestors established. By the 1970s, however, the ethnic boundaries faded and our social circles diversified.

Yet some common threads always united us during the years from 1940 to 1975. We were always ready to fight for America, and the Greatest Generation secured victory in Europe and victory over Japan before returning home to establish a prosperity that carried the nation and Erie County through the entire period.

Subsequent generations answered the call to service in the Vietnam and Korean conflicts.

Downtown Sandusky was another common thread; a bustling retail and social center. We shopped at the Sears and the J.C. Penney stores, the five and dimes, Smith Hardware, Joseph's, Spector's, LaSalle's and dozens of locally owned boutiques and jewelry stores. We "cruised" up and down Market Street and Columbus Avenue, or "buzzed the avenue," as some called it, when gasoline was much cheaper than $1 a gallon.

We dined at Whitehouse and marveled at the Gar fish through the windows at Pelican Restaurant.

We went to movies at the State Theatre, the Plaza or the Ohio Theatre.

We gathered downtown to share the joys and disappointments of life. We celebrated V-E Day and V-J Day in downtown Sandusky, and it's where many marched in civil rights demonstrations.

We came downtown to hop a Cedar Point ferry for a quick dash across the Sandusky Bay to the amusement park we've always loved, or a Neuman Boat Line trip to Kelleys Island.

Manufacturing became king and brought a new General Motors plant to Perkins Avenue and a Ford plant on Tiffin Avenue. Industrial innovations were a staple of the waterfront paper district, where Hinde & Dauche was located. Our industries were intertwined, and manufacturing was the backbone of our economy.

Many of us chose factory work straight out of high school, where we were all but guaranteed a decent living and what we thought would be a job that could carry us through life and into a comfortable retirement.

Others chose higher education. College campuses from Bowling Green to the University of Cincinnati, and everywhere in between, were a destination for many.

We worked hard and played hard. We loved our high school sports teams, relishing the victories and bucking up our players when they fell short.

We were also passionate about the pros and shared in the glory when the Indians won the 1948 World Series and the Browns captured the 1964 national crown.

This book is dedicated to all those memories.

Matt Westerhold
Managing editor
Sandusky Register

PUBLIC SERVICE

The Axis Powers instilled Americans with a patriotic zeal that carried the nation into World War II and on to victory, and in Erie County it was no different. Our men and women returned home victorious and proud of the service they gave to their country and the world.

That patriotism carried over into the everyday lives of Erie County residents through public service in clubs such as the Kiwanis, the Lions and veterans service organizations that today all remain important parts of our society.

The ones lost are forever remembered and the ones who returned raised families, many very large by today's standards, and built an economy that was second to none. Honoring your country, the community and your friends and neighbors was the American way.

American Legion meeting, 1942. Alvin F. Weichel is standing with his foot on the side of the car. He was elected 13th District congressman from Sandusky in 1942 and took office in 1943. *Courtesy of Tom Gallagher*

Sandusky Police Department, 1940. Front row, left to right: Scotty Thom, Tom Ryan, Ed Dusold, Diz Grathwol, Chris Sehlmeyer, Chief Frenchy Bravard, Ed Smith and Henry Scherer. Middle row: Vic Adcock, Bob Traver, Curtis Krebs, Charles Bravard and Lawrence Gegner. Back row: Charles Fehr, Charles Vettel, Ben Buser, Paul Ringholz and Jack Darby. *Courtesy of Karen Gegner*

First fire truck designed for rescue calls, 1940. The truck was designed by the Sandusky City Mechanic. Left to right: Sandusky Asst. Fire Chief Clarence Owen, Sandusky Fire Chief Wilson McLaughlin, City Manager Karl Kugel and the Sandusky City Mechanic.

Courtesy of Jim Wichman, Sandusky Fire Department historian

William "Bill" Bickley, DeWitt Avenue, Perkins Township, dressed in his uniform for a parade, circa 1940. He served as a Marine in the Argonne Forest in France during World War I. *Courtesy of Betty Mingus*

Hospital at the Plum Brook Ordnance Works at Sandusky, Aug. 1, 1941.

Courtesy of Sandusky Library 80-5088C

First Erie County draft for World War II, Jan. 24, 1941. They are gathered on the steps of the U.S. Post Office at Washington Street and Central Avenue.
Courtesy of Sandusky Library HIGM-154

Scrap drive for the war effort at the foot of Columbus Avenue, 1942. The sign in front reads "Sandusky's plan to help Uncle Sam." Eisenhower medals were given to Boy Scouts who collected scrap metal.
Courtesy of John R. Daniel

James T. and John P. Malahy, 1943, were both participants in the Normandy Invasion of 1944.
Courtesy of Stephen J. Sartor

Norbert E. Boose, center, was the only local man who served in the U.S. Coast Guard aboard the U.S.S. Sandusky, a destroyer escort that patrolled in the South Pacific during World War II. The man on the left is Norbert's father-in-law, Edward M. Will; on the right is his father, Albert F. Boose. They are at 1511 Lindsley St., Dec. 12, 1942. *Courtesy of Edward Albert Boose*

Sandusky area recruits during basic training at the U.S. Navy Training Station, Great Lakes, Ill., 1943. Front row, left to right: Jim Lange, Clarence "Lefty" David and Jim Coleman. Back row: Art Ziemke, Commander James, Chuck Gundlach and Bob Blakely. *Courtesy of Clarence David*

Ralph, Eleanora and Art Sehlmeyer, January 1944, in front of the family home at 618 McEwen St. *Courtesy of Gary R. Mussell*

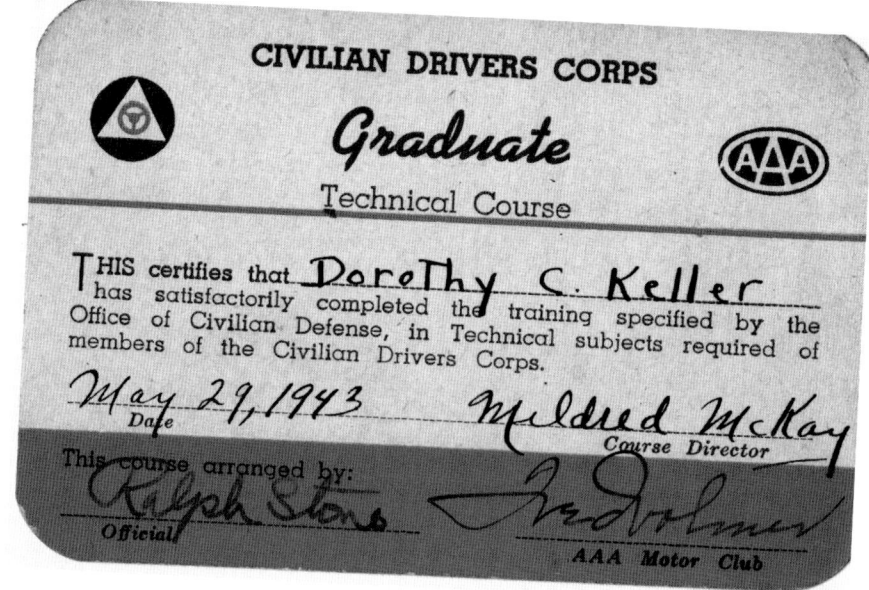

Civilian Drivers Corps card that belonged to Dorothy Keller, 1943. *Courtesy of Sandusky Library*

John C. Bahnsen Jr., U.S. Navy, with fiancée Ruth Steinhauser, circa 1945. They were married in June 1946.
Courtesy of Merita R. Wright

MEN & WOMEN

ASK YOURSELF
DO I HAVE AN ESSENTIAL JOB?
AM I EMPLOYED IN WAR WORK?

IF YOUR ANSWER IS "NO"

We Have A Job For You

YOU ARE NEEDED IN

WAR PRODUCTION

IN SANDUSKY

OUT OF TOWN JOBS ALSO AVAILABLE

TRANSPORTATION PAID TO JOB OUT OF TOWN — HOUSING GUARANTEED

YOU WILL BE HIRED AT ONCE!

DIRECT HIRING at YOUR BEST SKILL

May 22-23 8 A.M. to 8 P.M. May 24-25 8 A.M. to 5 P.M.

U.S. Employment Service

182 East Market Street — SANDUSKY, OHIO

Job recruiting poster during World War II, circa 1942. *Courtesy of Sandusky Library*

Boy Scout group at the Erie County Children's Home, June 1944. Front row, left to right: unidentified, John Garlock and Carl Hallio. In back are Raymond Schell and Curtis McKarty. *Courtesy of Sandusky Library SEGR-391*

World War II ration book belonging to Helen Hansen of Sandusky, 1943. *Courtesy of Sandusky Library*

Sandusky area Navy recruits were shipped to the U.S. Naval Training Station at Great Lakes, Ill., for basic training. Clarence "Lefty" David is second from the right in the second row from the top. He was pulled from this group to become a cook on a ship. Other recruits from Sandusky include: Bob Blakely, Jim Coleman, Chuck Gundlach, Art Ziemke and Jim Lange. *Courtesy of Nancy Hodges*

World War II Marine Franklin Steinhauser, 1943.
Courtesy of Merita R. Wright

Sandusky Fire Department in front of Station No. 3, June 1944. Left to right: Lt. Donald Hankamer, Capt. Frank Wilk, George Albert, Chief Wilson McLaughlin, Andy Seitz, Robert Slyker and Larry Gassman. *Courtesy of Sandusky Library SEGF-240*

PUBLIC SERVICE

Safety Town organizers, 1948, left to right: Vic Adcock, Carl Stevens, unidentified and Richard Smith with two children who attended. *Courtesy of Mary Papenfuss*

Carl "Tex" Neese served in the U.S. Navy, 1945. *Courtesy of Deborah Neese Voltz*

Louis Michel, left, and John Daniel on completion of boot camp at Great Lakes Naval Training Center in Chicago, May 1952. The two were friends from the first grade. *Courtesy of John R. Daniel*

Junior hostesses of the Erie County U.S.O. Center at their last party, held at Plum Brook Country Club, 1945. The U.S.O. Center was at the rear of the Lake Shore Depot on Columbus Avenue and was established in September 1942. Front row, left to right: Ruth Harten, Mary Ackerman, Lois Zank, Alice Bates, Catherine Martin, Janet Kuhn, chairwoman Mary McCann, Margie Fox, Helen Aldrich, Katherine Sidell, Pat Reckinger and Evelyn Missioni. Second row: Mary Homegardner, Pat Wolverton, Eleanor Donahue, Pat Leininger, Dorothy Wolverton, Grace Leininger, Sylvia Hein, Ruth Garrett, Doris Mielke, Dorothy Fisher, Edith Sidell, Phyllis MacDougall, Pat Gilbert and Rita Herzog. Third row: Eleanor Sinerson, Esther Popke, unidentified, Lenore Bossetti, unidentified, unidentified, Helen Louise Reeme, Marjorie Martin, Mary Beth Bryant and Julia Powell. Fourth row: Ruth Wiesler, unidentified, Lowell Schnecke, Florence Shuffle, Ruth Jean Kastor, Margaret Geigel, Marge Schott, Jean Appell, Luella Hein, Mary Daniel and Winifred Wetzler.

Courtesy of Sandusky Library CLUB-167

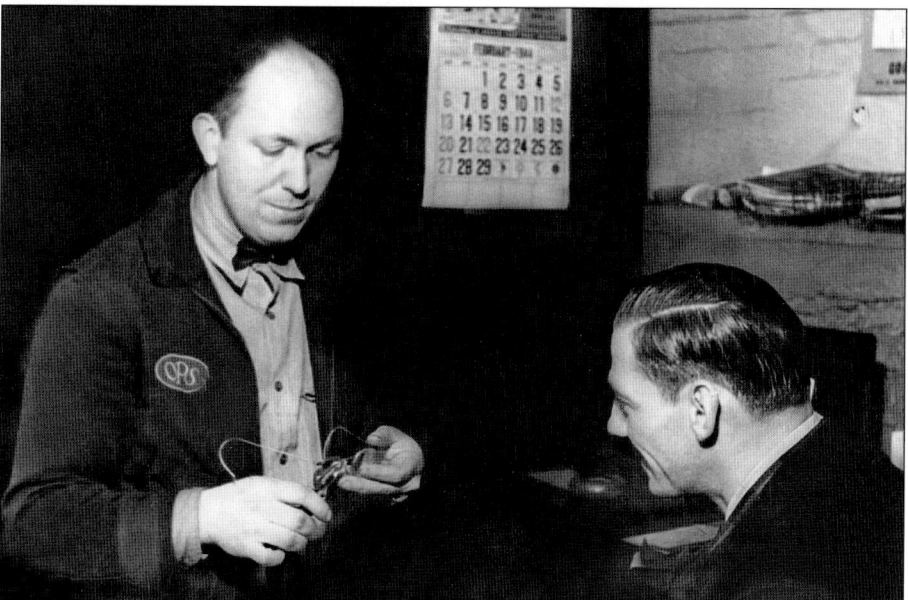

R.C. Gegner working at the meter shop of Ohio Public Service, 922 W. Water St., 1944. *Courtesy of Karen Gegner*

Sandusky Fire Department gathered for Field Day in Central Park, 1944. Front row, left to right: Norm Windisch, Capt. William Herb, Alfons Boesch, Andy Seitz, George Hanson and Lauton Seitz. Back row: Asst. Chief Marv Johnson, Chief Paul Bing, Capt. D. Hankamer, Lt. Spier, Capt. Frank Wilk, Capt. El Waterfield, Chief William Lang, Al Hanson, Larry Gassman and Robert Slyker. *Courtesy of Sandusky Library SEGR-315*

city mechanic Chris Meyer, Asst. Chief Clarence E. Owens, city electrician Sam Bickley, George Albert, Capt. Wayne Martin, Asst. Chief Bill Collumb, Ed Veith, Capt. William Waterfield, City Manager Al Lauber, Chief Wilson "Slip" McLaughlin, Asst. Chief Glenn Rehfuss, Asst. Chief Alto Heinz, Capt. Charles Keller, Asst.

PUBLIC SERVICE

Erie County Garage employees, 1948. Left to right: Al Roeser, Ed Eckman, Fred Sartor and Whitey Schneider. The garage had previously been used to house interurban cars. *Courtesy of Donna Elmer Sartor*

Alvin F. Weichel, 13th District Republican representative to U.S. Congress, at his desk in Washington, D.C., February 1952. Weichel served as U.S. representative from 1943 to 1955. *Courtesy of Bob Weichel*

Ohio State Highway Patrol, Erie County Sheriff and Sandusky Police Department cars, circa 1950. *Courtesy of Karen Deitz*

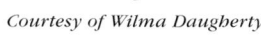

Fundraising drive for Good Samaritan Hospital, 1950.
Courtesy of Wilma Daugherty

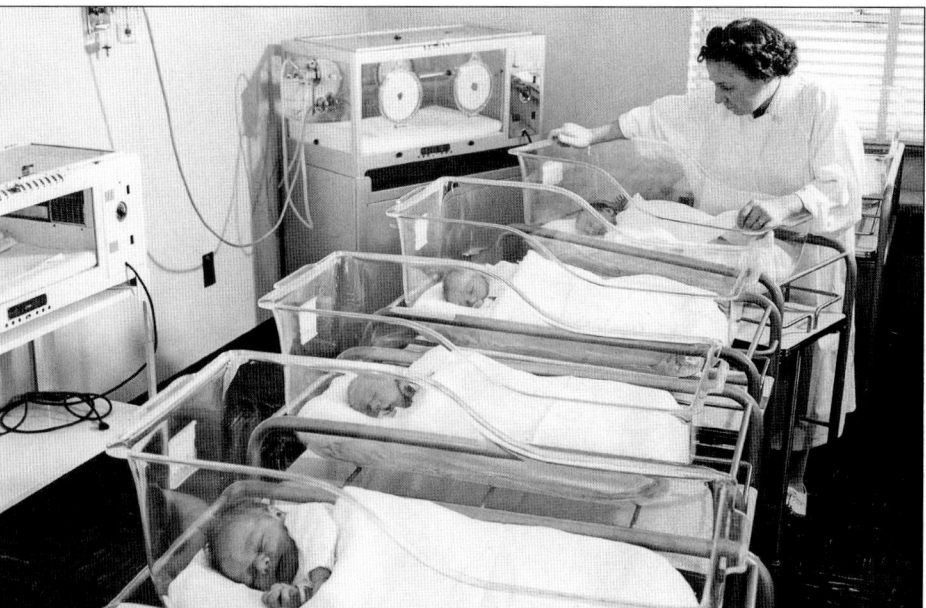

Obstetrics department of Sandusky Memorial Hospital, 1953.
Courtesy of George L. Mylander

Joseph Michel, city park supervisor, at the Sandusky city greenhouse, 1952.
Courtesy of Lynn Montelauro

PUBLIC SERVICE

Nurse capping ceremony at Providence Hospital School of Nursing, 1954. *Courtesy of Betty Mingus and Stephen J. Sartor*

Open house to celebrate the opening of Sandusky Memorial Hospital, Hayes Avenue, Oct. 31, 1953. From left to right: Dr. James Walker, hospital trustee; John Kerchner, hospital trustee; nuns from Providence Hospital; Dr. Lester Mylander, hospital trustee and founder; Rudy Knauer, Sandusky mayor; Mrs. Christine Mylander; Harold Schaeffer, city commissioner; Luther Heiserman, hospital trustee and William Maschael, hospital administrator.

Courtesy of George L. Mylander

View of the Erie County Jail on Adams Street, April 12, 1954. The Sandusky Library is at the far left. *Courtesy of Sandusky Library SEGR-057*

PUBLIC SERVICE

Looking toward the U.S. Post Office in Sandusky, March 6, 1957.
Courtesy of Sandusky Library SEGR-288

Mary Eloise Evans, the first woman in the Erie County Sheriff's office, February 1958. *Courtesy of Sandusky Library SEGR-80*

Dedication of the City Building on Meigs Street, May 4, 1958.
Courtesy of Sandusky Library SEGR-352

John Huston, left, and Mark Volz receiving awards for Safety Patrol from Officer Del Seiler, 1963. Mark went on to become a Sandusky police officer. *Courtesy of Bob and Barb Volz*

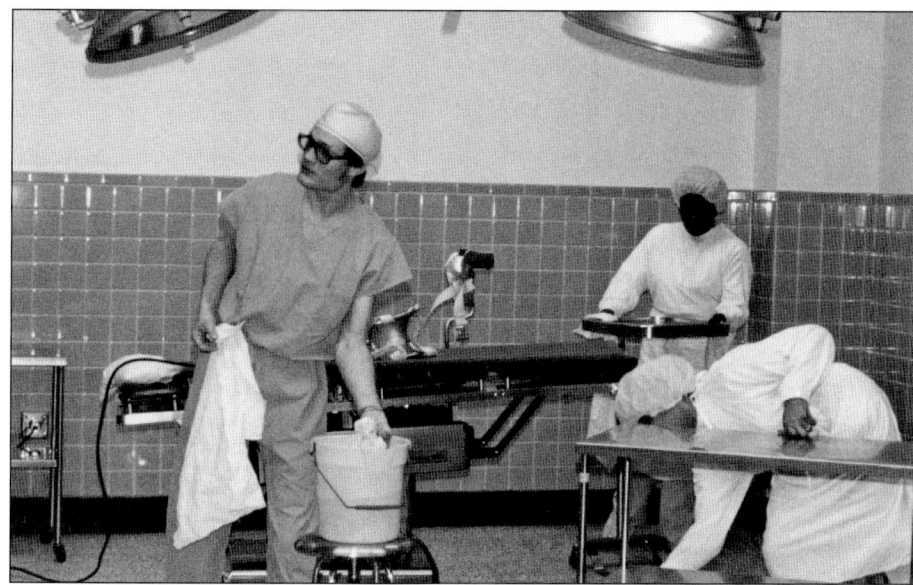

Cleaning an operating room surgical suite at Good Samaritan Hospital, 1975. Housekeeping employees, left to right: Donald LaCourse Jr., Lisa Pace and Ernie Turner. *Courtesy of Donald LaCourse Jr.*

Amy and David Weichel sitting on the running board of a 1937 Ahrens-Fox fire engine on Columbus Avenue in front of Gray Drug, August 1975. They are participating in the Annual Firemen's Shoe Fund collection. *Courtesy of Bob Weichel*

Providence Hospital Gray Ladies, circa 1975. The lady third from the left in the back row is Helen Norberg. *Courtesy of Donald P. Schlett*

CELEBRATIONS

Erie County had plenty to celebrate in the three decades following the end of World War II.

And celebrate we did.

When Sandusky had a year-long party to mark its Sesquicentennial in 1968, it was easy to tell which of the city's men were caught up in the hoopla. They wore their hearts on their sleeves and beards on their faces to show their loyalty to their hometown — and to win top honors in the Sesquicentennial Beard Contest.

The area nearly burst with pride when Jacquelyn Jeanne Mayer brought home the Miss America 1963 crown. The *Sandusky Register* put out a special publication to mark the event. The high point came when Columbus Avenue was lined four-deep with well-wishers for the "Welcome Home, Jackie" parade. High school bands and marching units from across the state joined queens and their courts from small-town festivals and county fairs to pay homage to the fairest of them all — our own Miss America.

Times may change, but as long as flags are waving at the front of Memorial Day parades, high school football teams and marching bands are charging up local stadiums and Santa finds his way each year to the Cookie House in Washington Park, Erie County has much to celebrate.

Homecoming parade in Sandusky for Jackie Mayer, Miss America 1963. More than 80,000 people watched the parade to welcome her home. *Courtesy of Jackie Mayer*

Grape Festival Parade in Sandusky, Sept. 1, 1940. *Courtesy of Sandusky Library SAPI-249*

Grape Festival Parade on Columbus Avenue, Sept. 1, 1940. *Courtesy of Sandusky Library SECM-254*

Grape Festival Parade on Columbus Avenue, Sept. 1, 1940. *Courtesy of Sandusky Library SECM-261*

The Ice Queen seated at Battery Park during the Ice Carnival in Sandusky, 1941. *Courtesy of Sandusky Library SAPK-021*

Navy Day parade on Columbus Avenue, November 1945. The men on the float represent the five men raising the American flag on Iwo Jima.
Courtesy of Evelyn Zeller

All Ohio Veterans Day parade in Sandusky, Aug. 3, 1946.
Courtesy of Sandusky Library SAPI-252

Float in a Sandusky Armed Forces Day parade, May 20, 1950. The man on the truck with the officers is Frank Nims, who was blind, and is "reading" the bell. *Courtesy of Sandusky Library SAPI-033*

Neighborhood Fourth of July parade on 1310 W. Madison St., 1950. Front row, left to right: Jackie Keller, Carol Fenton, Marilou Fenton and Joy Joliff. In back are Amelia Fenton and Judy Johnson. *Courtesy of Amelia Fenton Davlin*

CELEBRATIONS

Shriner parade at the corner of East Market and Wayne streets, circa 1955. Duane Elmer is leading the group. *Courtesy of Donna Elmer Sartor*

Parade in front of the Milan Police Station, 1965. The 1927 American La France fire truck, owned by Don Likes, is driven by Adam Sternberg. *Courtesy of Annette Likes Ramey*

Homecoming parade for Berlin Local School on Center Street, 1959. Ron Vaughan is driving the Farmall tractor with a float for Boy Scout Troop 236. The scouts are following with Eugene Vaughan, scout master, on the right of the troop. *Courtesy of Becky Coleman*

Clowns during a circus parade, circa 1962. On the left is Art McCall; on the right is Louis Dennis, both of Sandusky. *Courtesy of Mike McCall*

Driving through Cedar Point for Miss Ohio Day, 1962. Tom Griffiths from KYW-TV is in the convertible beside Miss Ohio, Jackie Mayer. *Courtesy of Jackie Mayer*

Display of "Hats off to Jackie," Miss America 1963, at Ohio Electric Company, West Washington Row, November 1962. *Courtesy of Jackie Mayer*

Welcome Wagon display at Kresge's welcoming Miss America 1963, Jackie Mayer, November 1962. *Courtesy of Jackie Mayer*

CELEBRATIONS

Miss America Jackie Mayer in the homecoming parade on Hayes Avenue and Tyler Street, 1963.

Courtesy of Barbara Garrett

A Volkswagen decorated and "buzzing the Ave." to welcome Jackie Mayer home as Miss America 1963. *Courtesy of Jackie Mayer*

Limbo contest during Miss Ohio Day at Cedar Point, 1962. Jackie Mayer, Miss Ohio 1962, is wearing her sash. *Courtesy of Jackie Mayer*

Eaglettes Middies Color Guard in the American Legion parade, June 13, 1965. Starting third from the left: Ann Rogers, Kathy Hallock, Elaine Bostater, Jackie Senn and Vickie Riley.
Courtesy of Elaine Bostater

Band in the Sandusky Sesquicentennial parade, June 22, 1968.
Courtesy of Sandusky Library SECM-226

Laurie Lee Schaefer won the Miss Ohio Pageant at Cedar Point, 1972. She went on to claim the title of Miss America. On the left is Bob Zetler and to the right are Zep Porterfield and Natalie Marshall. *Courtesy of Judy Porterfield*

New Departure float in the Miss Ohio parade on Columbus Avenue, 1969.
Courtesy of Suzanne Johnson

DISASTERS

The July 4, 1969, storm that dumped nine inches of rain left residences and businesses underwater and stands out in everyone's memory. But there also were great floods in 1959.

Other disasters also brought neighbors together to help each other. The Great Thanksgiving Storm of 1950 dumped 10 inches or more of snow. It was the weekend for the classic Ohio State-Michigan game, with the Big Ten championship and a trip to the Rose Bowl on the line, and the matchup in Columbus became known as Blizzard Bowl.

Holidays seemed to be a marker for disasters, and April 11, 1965, another hit: The Palm Sunday tornadoes. Erie County was spared the deadliest winds, which killed 55 people across the state.

Boats adrift and both marinas under water at Huron the day after the July 4, 1969, storm that dumped nine inches of rain. *Courtesy of Tom Root*

Masonic Temple fire, Jan. 27, 1943.
Courtesy of Jim Wichman, Sandusky Fire Department historian

Train wreck at Huron Main Street crossing, June 5, 1947. The NYC Railroad engineer died, eight were injured and 11 interstate express coaches were derailed. *Courtesy of Charles Hartley*

Mr. and Mrs. Hanchen with their '58 Ford Fairlane at 410 W. Strub Road, flood of July 1966. *Courtesy of James and Judy Marshall*

Train wreck on Campbell Street, 1967. *Courtesy of Suzanne Johnson*

DISASTERS

Fire at W.W. Woolworth Co. on Columbus Avenue, Jan. 5, 1960. Eight fire fighters were hurt, including Perkins Fire Chief Sartor.
Courtesy of Jim Wichman, Sandusky Fire Department historian

Bob Guss Jr. and his sister, Connie, at the flooded Camp Street underpass during the flood, July 4, 1969. *Courtesy of Robert Guss Sr.*

Hayes Avenue flooded in July 1969. *Courtesy of Suzanne Johnson*

St. Stephen United Church of Christ, 905 E. Perkins Ave., looking east. Pipe Creek flooded its banks pouring up to six feet of water in the church, July 4, 1969. *Courtesy of Janis Grathwol Burke*

McDonald's, 1934 Cleveland Road near Pipe Creek, under water during the July 4, 1969 flood. The freezer floated away in the floodwaters, but the business was able to reopen in three days. Mr. and Mrs. Warren Armstrong were owners of the first McDonald's in Sandusky from 1962 to 1974. *Courtesy of Mr. and Mrs. Warren Armstrong*

RELIGION

Churches played a major role in our lives. We attended services on Sunday mornings, but also came back for Bible study or prayer meetings on Sunday and Wednesday nights. There were no school activities scheduled on Wednesday evenings so students could participate in church activities.

In 1950 Sandusky had 31 active churches representing 21 denominations. Many had to expand their facilities or build new ones as the Baby Boom swelled attendance in Sunday school classes.

Churches were a place where we celebrated life's milestones, from births and baptisms to first communions to weddings and, finally, to funerals. There was no better place to eat than the church potluck, where women proudly shared their favorite dishes.

First service and dedication of the new building of St. Stephen United Church of Christ, 905 E. Perkins Ave., Christmas Eve, 1964. Rev. Clarence W. Kohring led the congregation. *Courtesy of Janis Grathwol Burke*

Confirmation class at Trinity Lutheran Church in Venice, 1944. The minister was Rev. John Braun, who was also a chaplain for the United States Armed Forces in the European Theater during World War II. Seated in the front row, left to right: Elmer Wahl, Wayne Orshoski, Joyce Galloway, Betty Martin, Rev. John Braun, Joyce Gardner, Nancy Klafter, Donald Orshoski and Rolland Orshoski. Back row: Norm Oeder, Richard Quinn, Marilyn Martin, Albert Oeder, Paul R. Orshoski, Stan Perry and Curtis Miller. *Courtesy of Joyce Orshoski*

RELIGION

Confirmation class of Zion Lutheran Church, 1941. Rev. Theodore Stellhorn Jr. is on the left in the front; Rev. Theodore Stellhorn Sr. is on the right. Charles W. Bostater is in the first row of boys second from the right. *Courtesy of Elaine Bostater*

Grace Episcopal Church on the corner of Washington and Wayne streets before the steeples were removed, 1942. *Courtesy of Bob and Barb Volz*

Erie County Ministers Association at New Departure plant, April 17, 1951. Al Herold was the manager. Rev. Robert Frey is on the top of the table on the right. *Courtesy of Matt Frey*

Confirmation class, Zion Lutheran Church, circa 1942. The pastors are Rev. Stellhorn Sr. and Jr.; Marilyn Gast is sixth from the right in the front row. *Courtesy of Brenda Bahnsen*

Holy Angels Church first communion, May 1952. Front row, left to right: first four are unidentified, Marie Polta, Mary Hurak, unidentified, unidentified, Linda Lange and unidentified. Second row: Jim Crooks, Norm Derrick, unidentified, Paul Blade, Tim O'Brien, unidentified, Rudy Decaro, Dave Dahnke, John Tucker, unidentified and Jim McCormick. Third row: Leroy Gast, Rich Cross, six unidentified and Terry Barrett. Fourth row: Ken Yontz, Jack Olds, Walt Agsten, unidentified, unidentified, Tim Reardon, Jim Mutz and Charles Schlict. Back row: Ken Yontz, Ed Boose, Nick Denslow, Ralph Cruz, unidentified, Clarence Kochensbarger and unidentified. *Courtesy of Edward Albert Boose*

RELIGION

First communion class of 1955 at St. Mary's School. *Courtesy of Stephen J. Sartor*

Confirmation at St. John's United Church of Christ, Milan, circa 1960. Front row, left to right: David Weilnau, John Weilnau, Dennis Weilnau, Gail Schaefer, Sheila Conway, Diane Deering and Judith Leber. Back row: Delbert Gittinger, Tom McAllister, Jean Best, Sandra Smith and (unknown) Klaholtz. Rev. Edgar Shelly is in the back. *Courtesy of Brenda Bahnsen*

Confirmation class of St. John Lutheran Church in Groton Township, Ohio 99 near Strecker Road, 1960. Front row, left to right: Judy Hildebrand, Lois Reynolds, Cynthia Sargeant, Bonnie Woessner and Betty Jean Nixon. Back row: Martha Weisz, Richard Sargeant, Roger Dickman and William Davis. *Courtesy of Roger Dickman*

Confirmation class of St. Stephen United Church of Christ, April 1955. Front row, left to right: Sue Koegle, Amelia Fenton, Thelma Starkey, Sandra Ohlemacher, Carole Hudson, Roberta Cassidy, Nancy Hoddick and Joanne Edwards. Second row: John Bremer, Charles Mayer, Keith Knauer, Ronnie Riccelli, Wayne Daniels, Jim Brinker and Richard Hire. Back row: Rev. Richard Belsan, Ronnie Camp and Jack Wilke. *Courtesy of Amelia Fenton Davlin*

EDUCATION

The new Sandusky High School was built in 1955 at Hayes and Perkins avenues and the old high school became Adams Junior High. The location of the new SHS, near the Sandusky-Perkins Township border, was selected so it could also serve families living in Perkins Township.

But a merger of the two districts was not to be, and in 1957, the Perkins school district built its own new high school off Campbell Street in the township.

There was a merger of the Margaretta and Townsend school districts, the Bellevue Schools absorbed the York school district and the Berlin and Milan school districts joined forces. The Clyde and Green Springs districts also merged. All four mergers stand to this day.

The Sandusky Schools took pride in all its public school buildings and maintained the architectural excellence of each one through the years. Monroe School and Campbell School in particular retained that excellence through the years.

In the 1960s, residents pushed for Bowling Green State University to establish a branch campus in Erie County and rallied to raise enough local funding to convince the college to build. Some of the first Firelands College classes were held at Sandusky High School before the branch campus off Rye Beach Road opened in 1968.

Sandusky High School, 1940. First row, left to right: Patricia McRitchie, Rose Patton, Christine Roesch, Eleanore Perry, Betty McGowan, Rosemary Meyers and Ruth Otto. Second row: Ruth Metz, Marilyn Palmer, Mary Taylor, Jean Oswald, Harriet Riggs and Mary Brengartner. Third row: Jack Moots, John Schaefer, Robert Opfer, Walter Opfer, Carl "Tex" Neese, Virgil Young and Frank Papenfuse. Fourth row: Charles Fuchs, Robert Jamison, Everett Miller, Donald Gundlach, Earl Mayer and James Keller. Fifth row: Albert Paone, Robert Schnell, Richard Rausch, Kenneth Gast, John Harris and Eugene Miller. Back row: teacher Mr. Fleming, Leonard Cocherell, William Cole, Donald DeLor and Earl Christiansen. *Courtesy of Deborah Neese Voltz*

Sandusky High School A Cappella Choir, 1940. Maynard Furst is second from the left in the back row. *Courtesy of Delight Heckelman*

Mrs. Isaacs' kindergarten class at Osborne School, 1940. Front row, left to right: Carl Schott, Marilyn Ann Brinnon, Robert Strach, Margaret Ann Eberle, Paul Gibeaut, Charmaine DeMay, Mary Lowey, Jack Dutton, Alice Mary Ortman, Mary Ann Lauber and Barry Mitchell. Top row: Mrs. Isaacs, Joe Roesch, Bob Wyatt, Joan Johnson, Judy Speers, Eleanor Zeiher, Helen Jean Granfield, Sandra Sue Raha, Jack Moyer, Jack Stickradt and Lois Ann Hartung.
Courtesy of Judy Porterfield

EDUCATION

Third grade, Perkins School, 1940-41. Winifred Keller was their teacher. *Courtesy of Robert Delius*

Grade school class of Sandusky schools in front of Campbell School, circa 1942. Joan Groesch is in the second row middle. *Courtesy of Sheila Pfanner*

Sts. Peter and Paul School students, grades one through eight, 1940. Delight Ann Furst, second grade, is in the middle of the second row. *Courtesy of Delight Heckelman*

Perkins Elementary School sixth-grade class, 1943. In front are Tom Sartor and Bill Mayer. Front row, left to right: Betty Didion, Paul Schenk, twins Roger and Dwayne Gerold, Earl Likes, Bob Delius, Frankie Peterson, James Spencer, Gordon Locke and Joseph Corso. Included in the second row: Donna Jean Elmer next to the railing, Margaret McKinney with her arms crossed, Leola Irby, Florence Pate, Marilyn Rickard, Betty Papenfuss, Pat Neu, Judy Forest, Phyllis Bruhou, Pat Backman and Ruth Hehrer.
Courtesy of Donna Elmer Sartor

Home economics child care class at the Follett House conducted by the Sandusky High School, circa 1943. Left to right: Jenny Stellhorn, Elizabeth Killoran, Sharnee Lux, David Wright, Roger Haulblin, Johnny Myers, Johnny Rehfus, Lewis Seidner, Ellen Seamen, Nancy Blough and Martha Evans.
Courtesy of Sandusky Library SASC-268

EDUCATION

Sandusky High School Band on a picnic in Lions Park, summer 1944. The boy in the center of the back row is Joe Buder. In front of him in the center row in the flowered print is Marilyn Gast. To her left is Jean Hoffman. *Courtesy of Brenda Bahnsen*

Eighth-grade class at St. Mary's School, 1946. Sister Mary Laurenta was their teacher. Seated in the front row, left to right: Lawrence Schell, Edward Andres, James Grathwol, Harold Higgins, Marilyn Chamberlain, Estelle McFarland, Paulette Westerhold, Elaine Meyers, Shirley Krebs and Mary Louise Riedy. Second row, standing: Richard Kramer, Charles Bauer, James Thorpe, Paul McGuire, Ronald Kluding, James Beverick, Richard Grundler, Nickolas Pasqualini, Nancy Sass, Lois Naderer, Mildred Eschenauer, Dorothy Rumford, Shirley Foley, Mary Zeitzheim and Lucille Beat. Third row: Thomas Kenney, Harold Gisert, Frank Mouch, Louis Michel and Robert Fitz. To the left side between third and fourth rows are William Weltlin and James Westerhold. Fourth row: Walter Wagner, John Kiffer, John Viviano, John Daniel, Elizabeth Gurtz, Alice Riedy, Margaret Manner, Geraldine Kaman and Mary Sue Brand. Fifth row: Richard Ernsberger, Richard Wieber, Paul Smith, Mary Mantey, Rosemary Schultz, Mary Lou Krafty, Jean De Camp, Betty Erney, Rosemarie Davis, Patricia McFarland, Donna Schlett and Devera Moore. *Courtesy of John R. Daniel*

EDUCATION

First-grade class at St. Mary's Catholic School, Jefferson Street, 1946–47. Front row, left to right: Carol Pfanner, Mary Ann Eder, Barbara Mauch, Julia Casserly, Florence Whetstone, Thomas Galloway, David Mehling, Charles Flohr, Bryce York, David Chamberlin, Leo Kreidler and Sylvester Kramer. Second row: Betty Brogle, Sharon Brown, Joyce Lung, Carolyn Griffaw, James Keating, Robert Wiechel, Robert Scheel, Gene Brengartner, Chester Roesch and Donald Kaman. Third row: Judith Ritzenthaler, Jeanine Hugg, Rita Ringle, Juanita Sartor, Wanda Lorcher, Wilber Lorcher, Raymond Beat, Alois Tremmel, Ronald Krebs, Jerry Nickles and Ronald Zuber. Fourth row: Barbara Ostheimer, Barbara LeValley, Marjorie Crouch, Jerry Nolder, Tom Michaux, David Yeager, Dennis Winterhalter, Robert Reedy and Albert Hartlieb. Fifth row: Rosalie Forwalter, Jeanette Biechler, Jeanne Rader, Celeste Bonderer, Dan Yochem, David Haas, Ted Cassidy, Bernhard Hillenbrand, Earl "Ozzie" Reed and Thomas Erney. Sixth row: Susan Staley, Anita Brogle, Carol Tight, John Harkleroad, Michael Kluding, Paul Bischor, Michael Kresser, Eugene Harkleroad and Thomas Everett. Back row: Darlene Fischer, Carol Kieffer, Shelia Schwietzer, Marsha Schwerer, Judith Renwand, Dale Riedy, Eugene "Jack" Kaman, Franklin Rohde, Thomas Voltz, David Voltz and Robert Hippler (with tie). *Courtesy of Deborah Neese Voltz.*

Junior-Senior Prom, Huron High School, 1946. Front row, left to right: Betty Radzik, Elaine Meyers, Frances Tata, Carolyn Rau, Donna Lamb, Carmel Temper, Janet Bailey, Pat Detro and Audrey Specker. Second row: Irene Gurtz, Lois Hahn, Lina Lee, Jeanne Owen, Shirley Henderson, Pat Daugherty, Evelyn Legando, Catherine Meola, Marcella Wechter, Liz Christianson, Dorothy Slocum, Joanna Klein, Florence Beatty and Ida Henes. Third row: Margaret McCormick, Norma Meeker, Mildred Herber, Dorothy Dowell, Irma Bailey, Dorothy Brown, Mary Zimmerman, Dorothy Stefanik, Carolyn Meno, Edna Esposito, Catherine Frye, Theresa Temper, Mary Michel and Henry Lau. Back row: Kenneth Betsh, Kenneth Chicotel, Tony Gebelle, Sam Pisano, Ralph Washburn, Harold Wright, Wayne Jenkins, Tony Tata, Bill Shrigley, Don Gutzeit, Jim Lyons, Ed Asher, Bob Anderson, unidentified, unidentified, Karl Lynn, Harvey Klein, Bruce Donaldson, Don Wilford and Fred Wolfe. *Courtesy of Tom Hartley*

EDUCATION

Erie County School orchestra directed by Jim Hoffman, circa 1947. *Courtesy of Delight Heckelman*

Sandusky Junior High School class picture, 1948. Top row, left to right: Dick Kruse, Donna Markette, Don Miller, Jacky Fleming, Ron Skillman, Gertrude Welchons, Jerry Ehrhardt, Marion Osborn, Jimmy Dee and Nancy Smith. Second row: Ken Walton, Lata Hitchcock, James Larrick, Mayvell Conrad, Marge Anders and Bobby Gerlach. Third row: Joe Sidoti, Shirley Campell, Glenn Hoppe and Shirley Bickley. Fourth row: Elaine Alexander, Tom Gilkeson, Dorothy Kosel, Richard Gassman, Lucy Morrison, Willie Gibeaut, Virginia Kaltenback, Carl Schott and June Rattunde. Fifth row: Leon Blume, Janet Cremen, Vernon Barbour, Dianne Detlef, Peggy Conley, Nancy Byers, Jody Martin, Darlene Emerick and Nancy McPeek. *Courtesy of Shirley Bickley Cooper*

Madison School third-grade class, May 1949. Front row, left to right: Johnny Ferback, Rose Cane, Gloria Martin, Sandra Glass, Judy Smith, Delores Laplata, Carol Butts, Carol Meyers and Tommy Arthur. Second row: Paul Lyon, Tom Runkle, Larry Kaufman, Sandra Schatz, Nancy Webb, Karen Friedley, Joanne Edwards, Judy Morton, Judy Leibacher, Amelia Fenton and Lena Swain. Third row: Roy Lewis, Jim Gill, Jerry Leibacher, Charles Wright, Vincent Leto, Lowell Fritz, Mary Burger, Sharon Stimmel, Patricia Fink, Judy Keller, Thelma Starkey and Sally Sherrard. *Courtesy of Amelia Fenton Davlin*

EDUCATION

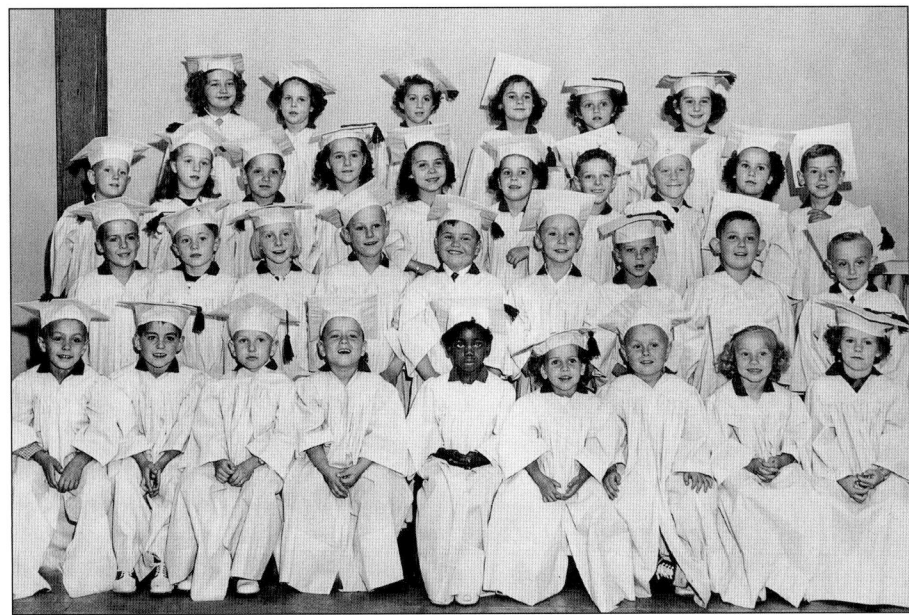

Cooperative kindergarten graduation, Campbell School, May 1948.

Courtesy of Karen Deitz

Huron High School, August 1949. *Courtesy of Tom Root*

Kindergarten class at Madison School, 1949. Included in the front row: Sue Frutig, Ann Wennes, Larry Weiss, Barbara Strickler, Bob Wassner and Marjorie Spector. Included in the middle row: Emmy Weis, Lynn Tanchon, Mark Holzapfel, Cheryl Smith and Joe Harbrecht. Included in the back row: Doug Swank, John Balconi, Tom Pascoe, Nicky Gordon and Nelson Hitchcock.

Courtesy of Barbara Garrett

Mrs. Wallace's kindergarten class at Osborne School, 1949. Front row, left to right: Joe Groscost, Butch Heim, Carolee Williams, Don Ebner, Patty Sharpe, unidentified, Jim Palmer, unidentified, Millie Trimarche, unidentified and Sally Meyer. Second row, fourth from the left: John Decker, Diane Hay, Ron Hlasten, Vicky Fazekas; on the end is Betty Unkrich. Third row, fifth from the left: Beth Mayer, unidentified, Dave Gibson, Dave Kahler, Bob Butler and Bob Wilke. Bob Disbrow is second from the right in the fourth row; Sandra Welty is third from the right in the fifth row. *Courtesy of John S. Decker*

May Festival at Osborne School, 1951. Penny Meyer (Raggedy Ann), John Decker (Raggedy Andy), Patty Appel (ballerina), Mimi Schwensen (dancer with headdress), Marilyn Miller (dancer with wand), Billy Purdy, Bob Disbrow, David Sharpe and John Vickers (tin soldiers). *Courtesy of John S. Decker*

Huron High School senior class play, "Cheaper by the Dozen," 1954. Joe Taylor is sitting on the floor. Sitting on the sofa, left to right: Clarence Hofer, Jim Fekete and Peggy Bean. Standing: Katherine Kaiser, Loren Leidheiser, Kaye McCormick, Nancy Steibly, Betty Bickley, Alan Sender and Jason Warren. *Courtesy of Betty Mingus*

EDUCATION

Sandusky High School A Cappella Choir in front of Adams Street School, 1944. Teacher Marion Willis is in the third row on the left. Also included are: Bill Newton, Bill Sheid, Jesse Bohanan, Richard Young, Gordon Ebert, Philip Gastier, Dawn Tripplet, Vera Dougherty, Lois Kaufman, Jean Trueman, Elenor Hill, Irma Berardi, Elenor Miller, Clem Bossiti, Jerry Denzer, Jack Ilsman, Don McGoorey, Kenneth Stephanz, Bill Beekan, Dale Griswald, Esther Lippis, Esther Blume, Alyce Anderson, Alice Polta, Joyce Corso, Jean Woodruf, Audry Bahnsen, Ileen Roth, Mary LaFace, Mary Herzog, Jean Bachman, Roth Palmer, Marilyn Thompson, Virginia Theim, Marcella Clemens and Richard Cline. *Courtesy of Richard Cline*

Graduation at Huron High School, 1952. Front row, left to right: Wanda Wittmer, Gene Thomas, Gene Tromblee, Nancy Burton, Dave Garton, Jody Laub, Harriette Pervis, Margery Barber, Marie Dalton, Janet Henes, Janet Orshoski and Verna Schell. Middle row: Don Ritzenthaler, Marianne McCormick, Lawrence Majoy, Bill Lyons, Barbara Wolfe, Don Lieb, Ruth Stamm, Rita Landoll, Dick Keefe, George Hermann, Carl Forthofer, Nelson Brownell, Trell Adams, Dwight Miles, Sam Detrich, Jack Farschman, Bob Dowell, Agnes Doyle, Gloria Esposito and Dottie McMillen. Back row: Shirley Steibly, Marilyn Yahn, Harry Wright, Bill Lusher, Shirley Leitz, Anita Sender, Gene Rhoad, Bob Tata, Barbar Phillips and Ed Chaffin. *Courtesy of Tom Hartley*

Ohio Wesleyan University men apply a new coat for Leo the lion before Leo's midnight ride back to the Sandusky waterfront perch in front of the Sandusky Yacht Club from which he had been abducted two years before. Left to right: Doug Paton, Andy Hull, Ronnie Rich, Gene Richter, Harold Craig, Cliff Aikens and Charles Craig. *Courtesy of Roger Dickman*

Monroe School choir Christmas concert in Center Hall, circa 1955. *Courtesy of Nanette Guss*

EDUCATION

Third grade at St. Mary's School, 1956. *Courtesy of Stephen J. Sartor*

McCormick School Annex seventh-grade class, Huron, June 1957. Front row, left to right: Miss Lucille Lynch, Norman Kurtz, Bill Boos, Janet Hughes, Alice Bellamy, Grace Hibbard, Janet Lipus, Mary Dunham, Doug Ricci, Bill Stoffer and Lester LaCourse. Second row: Jim Nesbit, Jerry Cunningham, Tom Craig, Mary Welchons, Betty Payne, Trudy Palmer, Trudi Hoak, Linda Green, Gary Savage and Dewey Neusome. Back row: Jim Boos, Ben Morrow, Ronnie Schuh, Bob Barnes, Ron Faller, David James, Don Hamler, Skip Humphry, Ed Boose and Jerry West. *Courtesy of Edward Albert Boose*

First group of Key Notes at Sandusky High School, 1957. *Courtesy of Karen Gegner*

EDUCATION

Frank W. Smith with a class of art students at Sandusky High School, circa 1950. He taught art and was known for his own work in watercolors.
Courtesy of Wilma Daugherty

The third-grade class of Venice Elementary School, 1959. Top row, left to right: Mrs. Margaret Hall, unidentified, Shelda Schweck, unidentified, Sharon Jackson, Bill Findley, Cindy Everhart, Leslie Dean and Lillian Salyers. Second row: Paul Fitz, Marylin Shumaker, Eddie Quinteras, John Liptak, Carol Church and Bill Bechstein. Third row: Patty Allen, Tom Keimer, Helen Hamilton, Dorene Orshoski, Rusty Meyers and Pauline Boyce. Fourth row: Howard Cousino, Marlin Kincaid, Richard Staugh, Anne Bertsch, Chuckie Wilson, Terri Timassy, Gary Merk, unidentified and Linda Hertlein. Fifth row: Cheryl Quick, unidentified, Debbie Milner and Kathy Welch. *Courtesy of Joyce Orshoski*

Board of Education, Perkins Public Schools, circa 1962. Left to right: James Hotchkiss; William Weagly, Erie County Superintendent; Nancy Pratt; T.W. Hartley, Perkins Schools Superintendent; Howard Lindsley; Dr. Francis O. Fry; Dr. H.L. Hoffman and Robert Koch, Clerk of Perkins Board of Education.
Courtesy of Tom Hartley

Groundbreaking for Berlin Heights High School, 1950.
Courtesy of Delight Heckelman

St. Mary's Cub Scout Pack 7, 1957. *Courtesy of Stephen J. Sartor*

Sandusky High School choir, 1957. *Courtesy of Karen Gegner*

Eighth grade at St. Mary's School, 1957. *Courtesy of Stephen J. Sartor*

St. Mary's School band, July 1960. John Talbot is their director. *Courtesy of Robert Delius*

St. Mary's School seventh grade, 1957-58. *Courtesy of Robert Delius*

Osborne Elementary School kindergarten class, 1973-74. The principal is Thomas Gallagher and the teacher is Renata Smith. *Courtesy of Deborah Neese Voltz*

SPORTS & LEISURE

The "Sensational Sixties" were perhaps the defining era for sports. From 1960 through 1969, the Sandusky High School Blue Streaks were known as the "Monsters of the Seaway".

The Blue Streaks finished with 87 wins, 10 losses and three ties under coaches Earle Bruce (1960-63), Bob Seaman (1964-65), Bob Reublin (1966-68) and Gene Kidwell (1969). Included were back-to-back 10-0 seasons in 1965 and 1966, and a 25-game winning streak that stretched from late in 1964 to early in the 1967 season. In fact, SHS teams won 38 games and lost twice in a four-year period.

Sandusky also won state championships in swimming (1946) and in golf (1947), and Sandusky's Thom Darden became the No. 1 draft pick for the Cleveland Browns in 1972 after a stellar college career at Michigan.

At Sandusky St. Mary's, standout Rich Davie set the high marks, scoring 2,001 points in his four-year basketball career (1966-1970), and he remains the only county athlete to reach that plateau.

The sport of high school wrestling in the county also surfaced on a state level In 1971. Huron High School had three individual state champions in finishing second in the team standings. Drew Gundlach (126), John DeLamatre (132) and John McGraw (175) captured crowns for coach Tom Talbott, and the growth of that sport has been remarkable since that moment.

Watermelon-eating contest at the Scott Paper Co. picnic at Lions Park, circa 1947. Ron Vaughan is second from the left; Dorene Vaughan is third. *Courtesy of Becky Coleman*

Dick and Bob Niehm ice boating on Sandusky Bay, 1940. *Courtesy of Clarence David*

Ice boaters on Sandusky Bay in front of the shanty they used to keep warm, 1940. From left to right: Paul Klott, Jimmy Weiland, Dick Niehm, Jim Roth and Clarence "Lefty" David. *Courtesy of Clarence David*

Arthur Lundgard, Arthur Lundgard Jr. and Louis W. Zeller after a successful rabbit hunt, Venice, 1940. *Courtesy of Evelyn Zeller*

Ice skating at Battery Park on Sandusky Bay, 1942. *Courtesy of Sandusky Library SAPK-017*

SPORTS & LEISURE

Noah's Ark attraction at Cedar Point, summer 1940. The left side of the building was Hilarity Hall, a fun house. *Courtesy of Bob and Barb Volz*

Harriett K. "Hedy" Schlessman at bat with her brother, Bill, catching, circa 1940. They lived on Patten Tract Road, Oxford Township, near Kimball. Harriett played second base on a women's team in Colorado during World War II and continued to be a life-long baseball fan. *Courtesy of Roger Dickman*

Picnic grove next to the Coliseum at Cedar Point, summer 1940. *Courtesy of Bob and Barb Volz*

Rockwell Trout Club at Castalia, circa 1940. *Courtesy of Sandusky Library NBRC-409*

Cedar Point Beach, summer 1940. *Courtesy of Bob and Barb Volz*

Louis Zeller with a prize catch in Venice where Cold Creek empties into Sandusky Bay, 1942. *Courtesy of Evelyn Zeller*

SPORTS & LEISURE

Races during the Ice Carnival in Sandusky, 1942. *Courtesy of Sandusky Library SAPK-018*

Jumping barrels during the Ice Carnival at Battery Park in Sandusky, 1942. *Courtesy of Sandusky Library SAPK-020*

A July 4th penny hunt on Chaska Beach at Huron, circa 1945. The annual event also involved nickels, dimes, quarters and fifty-cent pieces. *Courtesy of Tom Hartley*

Dan Neese with Helen and David Ehrnsberger at Cedar Point, circa 1950. *Courtesy of Deborah Neese Voltz*

This 1932 or 1933 Ford raced at the Sandusky Speedway, circa 1948. The chief mechanic was Ben Brownell. His son-in-law, Don Likes, is standing in front. *Courtesy of Annette Likes Ramey*

Ice skating at Battery Park, circa 1950. *Courtesy of Sandusky Library SAPK-053*

Carl Wilken Sr. and Jr. ice fishing for perch on Sandusky Bay, February 1953. *Courtesy of Jacob W. Wilken*

Ice fishing on Sandusky Bay, circa 1950. *Courtesy of Sandusky Library SECM-402*

Ice boats lined up for a race on Sandusky Bay, circa 1950.
Courtesy of Sandusky Library SECM-409

Kiddie Land at Cedar Point, circa 1952. Cousins Gayle Frankart and Duane Brownell are taking a ride. *Courtesy of Sue Coleman Frankart*

New Departure Hyatt golf outing at Mills Creek, circa 1955. Robert Schweinfurth is in the back with the print shirt. *Courtesy of Rich, Terri, Barb and Dave Schweinfurth*

Soldiers Home baseball team, 1954. Front row, left to right: Dick Volz, Bob Volz, Al Thorp, Jim Volz, Don Warner and Tom Hiss. Back row: manager Frank "Mike" Volz, John Parker, Hack Speer, Reed Fletcher, Jim Speer, John Bier, Lefty David, Norm Phiefer and John Parker. John Parker was the commandant at the Soldiers Home. After World War II many of these players formed a team put together and managed by Frank Volz. They played at the baseball field on the grounds of the Soldiers Home and provided entertainment for the veterans who lived there. This team stayed together and became Northern Ohio League champions for five consecutive seasons. *Courtesy of Bob and Barb Volz*

SPORTS & LEISURE

VFW basketball game, circa 1950. *Courtesy of Wilma Daugherty*

City baseball champions, 1952. Front row, left to right: unidentified, Harold Johnson, unidentified, Artie Gerold and John Knupke. Middle row: Dave Yeager, Larry Bender, Jim Thom, Ron Camp and Ed Will. Back row: Coach Gilbert, Dale Riedy, Dean Howman, Max Meridith, unidentified, Tom Voltz and unidentified coach. *Courtesy of Candia Howman*

Cedar Point viewed from the space spiral, circa 1960. *Courtesy of Suzanne Johnson*

Phillips 66 softball team at Battery Park, 1962. Front row, left to right: Tom Rudolph, Hal Burger, Tom Bertsch, Walt Long and Willis "Butch" Shively. Back row: Bill Arthur, manager Bob Thayer, Don Ebert, John Bragg, Ralph Sommers, Eldon Zimmer, Bob Boos and Fred Dahs. *Courtesy of Bill Arthur*

Raising the flag at Bay View Park baseball field, 1960. Left to right: Ed Grahl, Bill Wood, Herbert Hoelzer, Stan Greene, Bob Oakes, Bob Kohl and Paul Orshoski Sr. *Courtesy of Joyce Orshoski*

Beach party at Sheldon's Folly, 1968. Included are: Dean and Lorene Sheldon, Helen Jean Granfield, Judy and Zep Porterfield and Gail and Paul Mack. *Courtesy of Judy Porterfield*

SPORTS & LEISURE

Sandusky High School football team won the Buckeye Conference in 1966. First row, left to right: A. Keys, P. Cross, V. Malinovsky, W. Amison, B. Deming and G. Garrett. Second row: T. McNutt, J. Collins, R. Griffiths, B. Bravard, J. Reis and H. Lindsey. Third row: I. Amison, T. Catlett, D. Bloomquist, D. Copenhaver, W. Shaw and M. Nath. Fourth row: C. Lewis, L. Taylor, J. Rausch, E. Luckett, T. Pope and B. Ohlemacher. Fifth row: S. Morgan, P. Manuguerra, D. Agsten, T. Jenkins, J. Young and T. Wright. Sixth row: E. Williams, T. Darden, L. Grandberry, K. Krueger, D. Bragg and R. Newton. Seventh row: J. Jackson, J. Capizzi, Dave Maschari, M. Zimmerman, D. Miller and E. Zeigler. Eighth row: L. Richie, D. Wobser, M. Doctor, D. Castile, T. Seavers and J. Johnston. Ninth row: K. Michaels, L. Lay, R. Cuprys, D. Trimarche, C. Dent and T. Bloomquist. Tenth row: H. Shaw, R. Knighton, K. Smith, G. Schuster and D. Miller. Eleventh row, coaches: Flynn, Shields, Cauldwell, Norman, Juriga, Loffler and Reynolds. Twelfth row is equipment manager Deringer and coaches Kidwell, Reiber, Reublin, Currence and Vooletich. Thom Darden went on to a successful professional career with the Cleveland Browns. *Courtesy of Sandusky Library*

The first C.P. Hobo Band on the front porch of the Silver Dollar Cafe, Cedar Point, 1968. Bob Reardon is in front. Middle row, left to right: Bill Werner, Jeff Goodsite and John Hancock. Back row: Jack Deffenbaugh, Craig Otto, Bob Rogers, Ed Spayd, Dennis Chupa and Mike Newton. *Courtesy of Ed Spayd*

Sandusky rugby football club vs. Elyria rugby football club at the Rye Beach Road rugby field, Huron, fall 1973. *Courtesy of Ed Spayd*

Eagles Atom League All-Star team. The team representing the American League included: Alan Antel, Jim Roberts, Larry Chicotel, Sean Higgins, Bob Beekman, Milt Pritt, Chris Ackerman, Roy Patterson, Steve Cheek, Bryant Alexander, Bruce Reed, Mike Kasar, Bob Sennish, Bob Butler, Phil Dollard, Dave Johnson, Mike Thom, Kevin Ames, Tim Cottier and Jeanie Herold. They were coached by: Roy Patterson, Frank Ackerman and Tom Dupler. *Courtesy of Sandusky Library*

Sandusky rugby football club team on the rugby field on Rye Beach Road, Huron, fall 1974. Front row, left to right: Bob Gilbert, Mike Kline, Leo Koehler, Mike Nath, Bill Phipps, Jon Carver and coach Ed Spayd. Middle row: Jim Wolf, Gary James, Dave Ramon, Tom Nosse, Ken Zolinak, Mark Kastor, Toby Notestine, Dan Sartor and Paul Leslie. Back row: Steve Ritzenthaler, unidentified, Jim Hall, Keith Salinski, Mike Spayd, Chuck Smith and Mark Volz. *Courtesy of Ed Spayd*

The Lake & The Isles

Some things never change ... that much. The shores of Lake Erie always provided the respite sought on a hot summer day; Cedar Point always seems to have had thrill rides; and the islands offered that getaway from the hustle and bustle of life.

Walleye and perch were the catch of the day and beaches, boating and just plain fun always were on the menu. And the island wine was always sweet, or dry, depending on your preference.

Whether it was a Ford Tri-Motor flight or a Neuman Boat Line trip, the island paradises always beckoned.

For generations, the Sandusky Sailing Club and the Sadler Sailing Basin always had programs where young people could learn to sail, and the regattas provided a breathtaking view from along the shore.

All the while, the Lyman Boat Co. was producing the classic motorboats that still thrill.

Perry's Monument and Put-in-Bay Harbor, 1955. *Courtesy of Tom Root*

Vermilion-on-the-Lake beach, circa 1940. *Courtesy of Sandusky Library NBRC-508*

Commercial fishing dock, Kelleys Island, circa 1940.
Courtesy of Ted and Barbara Blatt

Kelleys Island boys playing football at Put-in-Bay, 1942. All the boys served in the armed forces during World War II. Front row, left to right: Charles Martin, Don Haig, Ted Bickley, Norbert McKillips, Jack Lange, Logan Bickley and Ralph Matso. Back row: Lester Colbert, Clyde Beatty, Claude McKillips, Ted Blatt, Lyle Bickley and Melbourn McKillips. *Courtesy of Ted and Barbara Blatt*

The *Pelee* ferry that operated from Sandusky, circa 1941.
Courtesy of Sandusky Library NBRC-158

Sandusky Sailing Club at the east end of Battery Park, circa 1940.
Courtesy of Bob and Barb Volz

Margaret Demante on the steamer *Put-in-Bay*, 1940. *Courtesy of Merita R. Wright*

Cabins on Lake Erie near Vermilion, circa 1940. *Courtesy of Sandusky Library NBRC-507*

Dick and Bob Voltz show off the pheasants they shot during a hunt on Kelleys Island, 1949. *Courtesy of Becky Coleman*

Sea plane in Sandusky Bay, 1947. *Courtesy of Sandusky Library TRAN-081*

Wine barrels at Kelleys Island, circa 1950. *Courtesy of Sandusky Library NBRC-349*

Lonz Winery on Middle Bass Island, circa 1955. *Courtesy of Roger Dickman*

Sandusky Junior Sailors, 1955. Left to right in the boats clockwise around the dock: Judee Harbrecht, Jerry Somerset, Rich Bing, Mary Feick, Lee Shadle, Butch Heim, Tony Tussing, Gary Harris, Frank Mouch, Harrison Pratt, Bobby James and Jim Root. Front to back on the dock: John Eschels, Vicky Schorger, Dave Mackey and John Decker. *Courtesy of John S. Decker*

Hunters at Kelleys Island standing in front of the Ford Tri-Motor, circa 1955. *Courtesy of Sandusky Library*

The *Challenger*, the 4-H escort boat to Kelleys Island 4-H camp, 1963. *Courtesy of Brenda Bahnsen*

Fly-in at Put-in-Bay airport with an overflow of planes on the east-west grass runway, 1958. *Courtesy of Tom Root*

Automobile and passenger ferry belonging to the Neuman Boat Line fleet operating between Sandusky, or Marblehead, to Kelleys Island, July 27, 1965. The corner of the Hinde & Dauch building is on the left. *Courtesy of Roger Dickman*

Lyman Boat advertising at the Sandusky Yacht Club, 1954. Judy Speers is in the bow of the boat with Joe Shepherd at the wheel. The man with his feet in the boat is Bill Parker.

Courtesy of Judy Porterfield

The "Tin Goose," a Ford Tri-Motor plane, arriving at Sky Tours Airport at Put-in-Bay with a group of winter anglers, circa 1965. *Courtesy of Roger Dickman*

Tourists at Inscription Rock on Kelleys Island, July 27, 1961. *Courtesy of Roger Dickman*

Seaway Marina blocked to boaters during a dispute on Kelleys Island, June 17, 1966. *Courtesy of Roger Dickman*

Charter fishing boat, the *Wahoo*, in Schrock's Marina, Lakeside, circa 1975. On board is Louis Zeller Sr., father of Douglas Zeller who owned the *Wahoo* and chartered many successful walleye fishing trips on Lake Erie. *Courtesy of Evelyn Zeller*

COMMUNITY

The Red Wagon popcorn stand and the Boy with the Boot are the icons of Sandusky, and great care was always given to Washington Park.

Music, from the Singing Grannies to the Chorale Society, and everything in between, filled the air, and proud parents supported the budding talents of young musicians in junior high school and high school bands just as much as any varsity football star.

Fairs and 4-H clubs kept young people busy, and unions helped keep people working and raised the standard of living across the county.

Local electricians, Local No. 867, put up Christmas lights for the city, circa 1945. *Courtesy of Richard Miller*

COMMUNITY

The Popcorn Wagon seen at the corner of Washington Row and Columbus Avenue, circa 1940. *Courtesy of Sandusky Library SAPK-244*

College Women's Chorus directed by Beverlie Mayer, far left, circa 1945. *Courtesy of Jackie Mayer*

Girls in front of a fountain at the Erie County Children's Home, April 1940. From left to right: Beverly Schell, Janice Erne, Elizabeth Ford, Alice Schaefer, Josephine Wheeler, and Gertrude Wise. *Courtesy of Sandusky Library SEGR-365*

Children at the Erie County Children's Home during the summer of 1942. *Courtesy of Sandusky Library SEGR-367*

Campers and counselors at Camp Fire Girls camp at Camp Kiloqua, Marblehead, circa 1942. *Courtesy of Judy Porterfield*

Sandusky Choral Society, circa 1940. *Courtesy of Sandusky Library ARTS-079*

Washington Park in Sandusky, circa 1940. *Courtesy of Sandusky Library SAPK-148*

The Boy with the Boot fountain in Washington Park in Sandusky, 1949.
Courtesy of Sandusky Library SAPK-117

Amassed high school band concert at the Sandusky Junior High School auditorium, circa 1940. *Courtesy of Sandusky Library SASC-409*

COMMUNITY

Hi-Y at the Sandusky YMCA, West Monroe Street, 1953. *Courtesy of Larry Showalter*

Washington Park in Sandusky, July 25, 1955. *Courtesy of Sandusky Library SAPK-176*

Boy Scout Troop 27 at the NW District Camporee at Milan River Campground, May 3, 1953. Front row, left to right: Gary Loe, Tom Runkle, Rich Leber, David Meyer, Tom Arthur and Rich Hire. Second row: Dennis Schwerer, Charlie Wright, Bill Arthur, Chuck Wilson, Jerry Liebacher, Ron Pendelton and Vince Leto. Third row: Tom Neumeyer, Dave Dutton, Phil Mazur, Dick Baker and George Bromm. Fourth row: Ned Bromm, Al Arthur and Tom Layton. *Courtesy of Bill Arthur*

4 Notes + 1 band, circa 1950. Tootsie Maschari is on the left; Jim Henry on the right. *Courtesy of Mary Papenfuss*

Float to represent the first Soap Box Derby in Sandusky, 1952. On the float, left to right: Mary Anne Ehrhardt, Rosemary Apel, Martha Maschari and Ray VanBlarcum Jr. *Courtesy of Ray VanBlarcum Jr.*

Camp Fire Girls camp at Camp Kiloqua, July 27, 1958. Counselors in the back row, left to right: Barb Little, Hap (unknown), Jane (unknown), Jane Gosser, Norma (unknown), Ann (unknown), Jackie Mayer, Anita (unknown), Mimi (unknown), Rach (unknown), Fran (unknown) and Elaine Moore. *Courtesy of Jackie Mayer*

COMMUNITY

Camp Fire Girls, 1953, left to right: Lynne Bromm, Beth Mayer and Wilma Sallee. *Courtesy of Jackie Mayer*

October meeting of the Martha Pitkin Chapter of the Daughters of the American Revolution, circa 1957. Seated, left to right: Mrs. John Wallers, Mrs. Ellsworth Rey, Mrs. Arthur Davis, Mrs. A.L. Opie, Mrs. G.A. Dauch, Mrs. Arthur Little and Mrs. R.P. Hankamer. Standing: Mrs. Edith Fast Grierson, Mrs. Edward C. Lay and Mrs. John Whitworth. *Courtesy of Sandusky Library 2005:5796*

Fifteen men won trophies in Huron's 150th anniversary beard-growing contest, Aug. 26, 1959. Front row, left to right: Donald Coleman, William Keating, George Fornoff, Charles Hofler and Carl Schuh. Back row: Karl Kramp, Howard Coleman, Jim Bryner, John Bartzen, John Bostater, Allen Slyker, Dick Drahos, Henry Hilbrook, Raymond Weyer and Frank Heimrich. Howard Coleman won the award for the fullest beard and John Bartzen for best halo beard. *Courtesy of Sue Coleman Frankart*

Sandusky Eaglettes majorettes, 1962, official marching unit for Miss America 1963 Jackie Mayer. They marched in the Miss America Parade, September 1962, in front of Jackie Mayer as Miss Ohio, then marched in front of her again as Miss America in September 1963. They raised money to travel to Atlantic City for both parades. Center, left to right: Diane Buck, Miss America Jackie Mayer and Gayle Green with Lori Zech behind. Kneeling: Charleen Allen, Tammy Moosbrugger, Dottie Andres, Sharon Ferguson, Sally Haar, Jean Sartor, Beckie Davis and Maggy Knerr. First row standing: Crystal Wobser, Cindy Pfanner, Sharon Yost, Doris Pitsenbarger, Linda Lichtle, Ann Nageott, Beth Bravard, MaryAnn McKenzie, Sandy Corley, Theresa McPeek, Denis Miller, Donna Kaman, Linda Ferback, Sheryl Watruba, Bonnie Richter and Laura Schmid. Second row: Libbie Stacey, Karen Mapus, Linda Kaman, Paula Dray, Phyllis Molnar, Marcia Camp, Kay Krebs, Linda VanCawenberg, Marlene Copus, Jean Ann Hirt, Sylvia Kramer, Lana Warren, Diane Cooper and Debbie Spring. Third row: Ken Canada, Jan Grathwol, Linda Streng, Nancy Furlong, Sueann Riccelli, Vicky Barnbrugge, Donna Ward, Debbie Moosbrugger, Kathy Jensen, Kathy Reynolds, Joy Jolliff, Susie Tunnington, Carol Kaman, Mary Beth Pfanner, Kathy Fox, Darlene Dunkel and Skip Hargrove. Guard: Jeanne Kromer, Patsy Furrer, Sara Geary, Judy Boos, Vicki Matter, Kathy Canada, Starr Webser, Linda Sandrock, Donna Lazara, Joyce Furbush, Rikki Kotz, Kathy Copus and Debbie Lazarony. *Courtesy of Janis Grathwol Burke and Jackie Mayer*

COMMUNITY

Line waiting to enter the Mills Bros. Circus, circa 1960. *Courtesy of Mike McCall*

The Erie County 4-H camp at Kelleys Island, circa 1958. The 21-acre facility provided summer camping activities to many campers over the years, including 4-H groups, scout groups and high school band practice camps. *Courtesy of Roger Dickman*

Wanita Washburn, a member of the Lake Shore Riders 4-H club at the Erie County Fairgrounds, 1960. *Courtesy of Sandusky Library CLUB-029*

"The Singing Grannies," 1970. In the front row, second from the left, is Mable Coffman. In the back on the far left is Geneva Harpster. *Courtesy of Donald LaCourse Jr.*

COMMERCE

It was a time before franchises when businesses of every kind were privately held and passed down from generation to generation. Father and son plumbing companies, electrical businesses, hardware stores and every other kind of retailer of the day were scattered across the county.

Even privately-owned shoe stores were abundant and when you walked in, the owner—or some member of the owner's family—would wait on you and probably knew your shoe size.

Retailing began to change in the 1950s with the advent of the Sandusky Plaza on Cleveland Road and later the Perkins Plaza on East Perkins Avenue. That set the stage for what would become the massive commercial strip along Milan Road. But if you drove out past the Old Soldiers and Sailors Home, what is now the Ohio Veterans Home, you were surrounded by farmland.

Smith Hardware Co., East Market Street, circa 1952, sold such things as appliances, televisions and household goods. The business closed in the early 1960s. *Courtesy of Charles J. Westerhold*

Front entrance of the Hotel Rieger, 1942. The front had been recently remodeled. *Courtesy of Sandusky Library BUSI-268*

Miller Drug store, 1033 Camp St., 1943. Pharmacist Otis Miller operated the business from the 1920s to 1970. *Courtesy of Dan Miller*

World's largest double streetcar diner on Perkins Avenue, circa 1945. The owner, Nat Sherrard, claimed to be the original promoter of french-fried onion rings. The business was later owned by the Berardi family. The Berardis started the first french fry stand at Cedar Point in 1942 along with owning and operating many of Cedar Point's first rides. Other Berardi family members ran the original waffle stand at the park. In addition to playing a big part in Cedar Point, the family has continued in the restaurant business in Sandusky, Huron and Norwalk. *Courtesy of Roger Dickman*

Trolley that became Jean's Diner on a flat car, 1947.
Courtesy of Sandusky Library BUSI-584

Roper Gas & Electric Appliances at 901 Columbus Ave., 1949.
Courtesy of Deborah Neese Voltz

Walter DeYo's drapery store, 1010 Hayes Ave. He purchased the store in 1947 from Seligers. *Courtesy of Mary E. DeYo*

Linn's in Battery Park, circa 1950. *Courtesy of Charles J. Westerhold*

Joseph Heiler, owner and operator of Heiler's ice cream parlor and grill at Ogontz and Third streets, circa 1950. *Courtesy of Candia Howman*

Interior of Frankie's Dairy Bar, 1950. Frank and Frieda Delius owned the establishment. *Courtesy of Robert Delius*

Feddersen-Smith Pastries display for a trade show in Sandusky, circa 1950. *Courtesy of Sandusky Library BUSI-390*

Ford cars and trucks on display in a park promotion for Sandusky Motor Sales, 1950. *Courtesy of Wilma Daugherty*

Advertising exhibit for Sunbeam Bread, 1950. *Courtesy of Wilma Daugherty*

Modern kitchen demonstration and cooking class at Smith Hardware Co., circa 1952. *Courtesy of Charles J. Westerhold*

COMMERCE

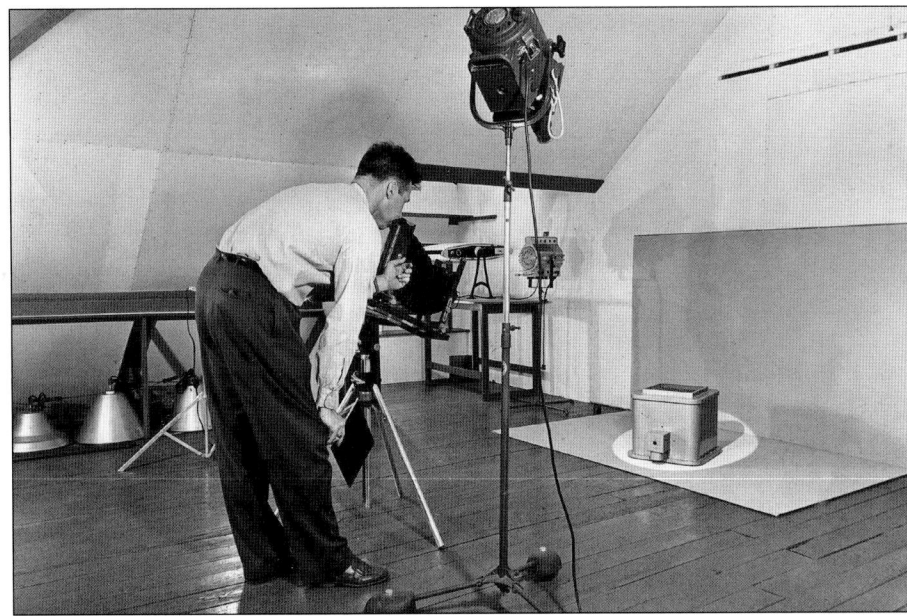
Bill Daugherty, a commercial photographer, in his photo studio, circa 1950. *Courtesy of Wilma Daugherty*

Exhibit for Sandusky Upholstering Co. at a trade show, circa 1950. *Courtesy of Wilma Daugherty*

Advertising exhibit for Curtis cabinets, circa 1950. *Courtesy of Wilma Daugherty*

Display of wines from the M. Hommel Wine Company of Sandusky, circa 1955. The company began in 1878. *Courtesy of Sandusky Library BUSI-633*

Charles Westerhold sits with customers during a demonstration at Smith Hardware Co., circa 1952. *Courtesy of Charles J. Westerhold*

Interior of Renande's Restaurant on the northeast corner of Perkins Avenue and Campbell Street, circa 1955. Mary and Leo Renande owned the family restaurant. *Courtesy of Roger Dickman*

George "Bud" Eldridge in his 1952 Chevy at the Dairy Queen in North Monroeville, 1954. *Courtesy of Wendell Blevins*

Nat Sherrard in front of his Skyway Restaurant on Cleveland Road East next to the airport, circa 1955. Nat was famous for Lake Erie pickerel and perch dinners. *Courtesy of Roger Dickman*

Jean's Diner, 501 E. Monroe St. in Sandusky, 1956. *Courtesy of Sandusky Library BUSI-585*

Evelyn Zeller at the opening of Evelyn's Cake Decorating Supplies at 5305 McCartney Road, July 1964. *Courtesy of Evelyn Zeller*

Rosa Mains, carhop at Skyway Restaurant on Cleveland Road, 1948.
Courtesy of Ed Spayd

Grand Opening at Miranda's Diner on U.S. 250 just south of Perkins Avenue. The restaurant was housed in a new stainless steel diner made to resemble an old streetcar. *Courtesy of Roger Dickman*

Industry

Erie County was fully engulfed by industry, and area workers produced everything from washers to dynamite. A strong back and a willingness to work was all anyone needed to get a full-time job at a decent wage.

There were box makers, crayon producers, builders, foundries, auto industry plants, boat manufacturers, lumber companies, brewing houses, rubber-based product makers and a whole host of other factories.

Making rubber gas tanks for B-29 bombers at Barr Rubber, 1943. *Courtesy of Sandusky Library BUSI-079*

INDUSTRY

J.W. Musson & Son Soap & Tallow Works, Pipe Creek looking south off Perkins Avenue, 1940. *Courtesy of Bob and Barb Volz*

Arthur Schlessman, on the cab, and his brother, Robert, at the original seed house of the Schlessman Seed Co. on the family homestead on U.S. 250 north of Avery, circa 1940. The young men were two of four sons of John Schlessman, the founder of the company. *Courtesy of Roger Dickman*

Raspberry pickers at the Schlessman farm on Patten Tract Road near Kimball, Oxford Township, July 1942. From left to right: Mae Laws Comparette, Leona Schlessman, Pauline Russell Druckenmiller, Verna Luttrel and Anita Heyl. *Courtesy of Roger Dickman*

Employees of the Lower Lake Dock Co. receiving turkeys for Christmas, 1941. *Courtesy of Richard Miller*

INDUSTRY

Scott Paper office staff, April 1945. Left to right: Evelyn Huber, Evelyn Weidenheft and Jean Spiegel. *Courtesy of Helen Schoewe*

Ladies from American Crayon Company, circa 1945. LaVesta Amolsch is in the second row on the left. *Courtesy of Sheila Pfanner*

Aerial view of Sandusky Foundry, circa 1945. *Courtesy of Wilma Daugherty*

Richard Spayd at the Raymond Brunow farm, South Hayes Avenue, 1949. Michael Babock is in the foreground. *Courtesy of Ed Spayd*

Two ore ships being unloaded by two Hulett unloaders at Huron, 1944. Eastern States Farmer's Exchange Elevator is under construction. *Courtesy of Tom Root*

Flower and vegetable stand run by August Corso Jr. and Grace Corso, 2073 Cleveland Road, 1950. The stand moved to that location from Hayes Avenue in 1944. Mr. Corso also sold vegetables and flowers from his truck around the Sandusky area. The next generation of the family continued the business. *Courtesy of Judy Corso*

Reed Bankert working on a washing machine at the Apex plant, 1950.
Courtesy of Mary Papenfuss

Hinde & Dauch Paper Co., corner of Mills and Madison streets, spring 1953. The straw stacks were for manufacturing corrugated paperboard.
Courtesy of Roger Dickman

Hinde & Dauch Paper Co. factory entrance off of Mills Street, April 1954.
Courtesy of Roger Dickman

Open house at the General Motors plant at Sandusky celebrating the production of the fifty-millionth car by GM in the United States, Nov. 23, 1954.
Courtesy of Sandusky Library 1996.5396

Western & Southern Life Insurance Co. picnic at Cedar Point, circa 1954. Deborah Neese is the third child in the train; Dan Neese the fourth. The girl waving is June Neese with Carl "Tex" Neese next to her. Herman King is the engineer. *Courtesy of Deborah Neese Voltz*

Helen Blevins in the pencil department at American Crayon Co., circa 1960. The machine, which Helen operated most of her employment, made China Mark pencils. *Courtesy of Wendell Blevins*

Charles F. Clark on his Farmall tractor in a cornfield on his farm known as "The Cedars" in Groton Township, 1955. It was located on Ohio 4 south of the Ohio Turnpike. *Courtesy of Roger Dickman*

Unloading iron ore at the Huron docks, 1955. The *J.H. Sheadle* ore freighter is being unloaded using the famous Hulett's machinery. *Courtesy of Roger Dickman*

Ore boats wintering at the Sandusky coal docks, March 17, 1957. *Courtesy of Tom Root*

Anita J. Cantelli next to a company truck loaded with concrete blocks, 1960. *Courtesy of Anita J. Cantelli*

Anita J. Cantelli loading blocks in the yards at Cantelli Concrete Block Mfg., Inc., 1960. *Courtesy of Anita J. Cantelli*

INDUSTRY

DuPont facility under construction south of Huron, June 24, 1962.
Courtesy of Tom Root

Westvaco handstitchers, Ruth Bradford and Mary Jane Cole, July 1965.
Courtesy of Suzanne Johnson

Aerial view of the Plum Brook 60 million-watt research reactor facility in Perkins Township, 1966. *Courtesy of Sandusky Library BUSI-172*

Assembling air filters at the Ford Motor Co. plant in Sandusky, 1968.
Courtesy of Sandusky Library BUSI-094

Entrance to the Ford Motor Co. plant in Sandusky, 1968.
Courtesy of Sandusky Library BUSI-096

Member of Laborers' Local 480, Perkins Avenue, 1970. *Courtesy of Betty Mingus*

Paul Wilken, Carl Wilken Sr. and Carl Wilken Jr. in front of Wilken Sheet Metal, 1107 W. Monroe St., summer 1970. *Courtesy of Carl Wilken Jr.*

Lyman Boat Works, 1615 First St., circa 1970. Lawrence Panzer is second from the left. *Courtesy of Jane Panzer Righi*

Steel slitter and automatic presses inside the Ford Motor Co. plant, 1968. *Courtesy of Sandusky Library BUSI-095*

Family & Friends

Clubs were king in the 1940 to 1970s era. A carryover from frugal entertaining of leaner times and with a nod to wartime brides' need to socialize among themselves while their men served abroad, canasta and bridge clubs, reading groups, sewing circles and progressive dinners were popular.

Not to be outdone, the returning soldiers sought out clubs where they could meet and socialize with their peers.

Fraternal organizations, veterans clubs and service associations flourished. Lions Club, Rotary, Elks, Eagles, VFW, Knights of Columbus, various Masonic organizations and scores of other clubs served as meeting places for their members and promoted good works within the community.

With a tavern on nearly every block in town and the burgeoning popularity of dining out, no one had to venture far to tap into good food, good spirits and the never-ending promise of a party.

For young people, socializing focused on school events, football and basketball games and, of course, buzzing the Ave.—a nightly ritual on the north end of Columbus Avenue in Sandusky. Introductions were made from cars at stoplights, new friendships were formed and young romances budded. Loathed by parents, police and downtown shoppers, buzzing was the social event of the era.

Ehrnsberger family at Ehrnsberger's Tavern on the corner of Decatur and Jefferson streets, circa 1945. Front row, left to right: Earl, Richard and Donald. Second row: Georgianna Ehrnsberger Rutger, William "Sonny," Robert, Geraldine and June. In the back row are Margaret Darby Ehrnsberger and William, the proprietor. *Courtesy of Deborah Neese Voltz*

Eileen Toft Stephens and Juanita Toft Sehlmeyer in front of the Toft home at 1413 W. Taylor St., 1940. *Courtesy of Gary R. Mussell*

Neighborhood bicycle parade on Wayne Street, 1940. From left to right: Helen Jean Granfield, Judy Speers, Jim McGuire, Bob Speers, unidentified and unidentified. *Courtesy of Judy Porterfield*

Birthday party for Carl Schott, May 1, 1941. Included are: Carol Schott, Carl Schott, Jackie Green, Jackie Voight, Mary Fenker, Joan Groesch, Jerry Granfield, Judy Granfield, Paula Squire and Sharon Squire. *Courtesy of Sheila Pfanner*

Group leaving for a Cleveland Indians game from the Schlessman farm in Oxford Township near Kimball, July 1942. From left to right: Bill Schlessman Jr., George Deering, Bill Erdman Jr., Fred Deering, Bill Erdman Sr. and Bill Schlessman Sr. *Courtesy of Roger Dickman*

Sisters Sharon, left, and Shirley Rutger on East Adams Street, 1944.
Courtesy of Deborah Neese Voltz

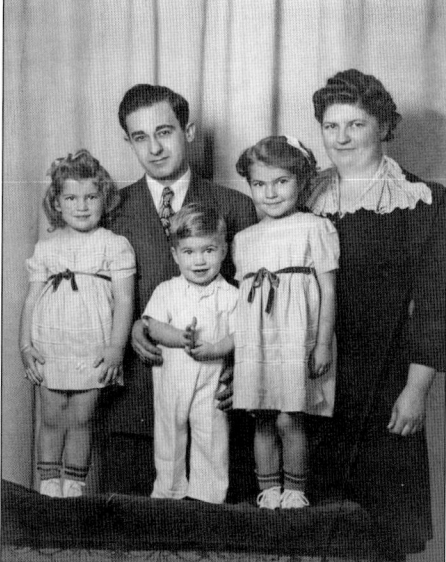

Carl and Bernice Hug with their children, left to right: Jeanine, David and Clarice, 1944. *Courtesy of Stephen J. Sartor*

Karen and Lawrence Gegner, 912 Fourth St., 1946. *Courtesy of Karen Gegner*

Marilyn Boose with son Edward, 1511 Lindsley St., February 1945.
Courtesy of Edward Albert Boose

Chuck, left, and Jim Corso on their father's truck, 1947. August Corso Jr. drove the truck around the area selling flowers and vegetables.
Courtesy of Judy Corso

Barbara Strickler, Bud Dobyns, Skip Roth and Sammy Renari playing in the yard of the Lions Park housing built for World War II veterans' families, 1947. *Courtesy of Barbara Garrett*

FAMILY & FRIENDS

Norbert Lange and Marion Cleaveland on the day they became engaged in 1945. They were both professors at Western Reserve University and he was a native of Sandusky and founder of Handbook Publishers, Inc., of Sandusky, a publisher of scientific textbooks. They funded the Lange Trust to provide for cultural enrichment for Sandusky residents. He died in 1970 and she in 1975.
Courtesy of Sandusky Library BIOG-266

Gary Hoelzer and Billy Rutger in front of the cotton candy stand at Cedar Point, 1948.
Courtesy of Deborah Neese Voltz

Reinhardt N. "Reiny" Ausmus, August 1946. A pioneer of aviation, he came to Sandusky in 1916 to work with Tom Benoist designing and building airplanes. He served in World War I, ending his flying career with injuries that left him with permanent disabilities. He was active in veteran affairs on the local, state and national level. *Courtesy of Jeffrey and Kimberly Smith*

Walter and Mary "Betty" DeYo with their 2-year-old daughter, Jeanne, 1313 Campbell St., 1946.
Courtesy of Mary E. DeYo

Joseph C. Michel family, 1946. Front row, left to right: Rita Michel, Mary Graves, Joseph Michel holding Joel Graves, Mabel Michel holding Lynn Graves, Paul Graves Jr. in front of Patricia Michel and Elaine Michel. Back row: Eugene Michel, Paul Graves Sr., Richard Michel, Helen McGuffin holding JoeEd McGuffin and R. E. "Mac" McGuffin. *Courtesy of Lynn Montelauro*

Carl and Mary Stevens on their wedding day standing in front of the Sandusky Park fountain, 1948. *Courtesy of Mary Papenfuss*

Emil and LaVesta Amolsch with Nettie Meunchow and Joan Groesch, Easter Sunday, 1950. The two ladies in the middle are the Zeitziem sisters. St. Mary's Church is in the background. *Courtesy of Sheila Pfanner*

Walt Bahnsen, left, and William Kahler, life-long Sandusky residents, May 1948. Walt worked as an electrician for the city. *Courtesy of Brenda Bahnsen*

Elsie and Joe Thurston on the east side of Columbus Avenue looking north, 1952. *Courtesy of Wendell Blevins*

Carl "Tex" Neese with children Dan and Deborah Neese at the Boy with the Boot Fountain in Washington Park, circa 1951. *Courtesy of Deborah Neese Voltz*

Bob, left, and Ron Vaughan from Berlin Heights visit Inscription Rock on Kelleys Island, Oct. 19, 1953. *Courtesy of Becky Coleman*

Sisters Gertrude Sharpe and Edith Temofaw, 1954. *Courtesy of Candia Howman*

Jim and Barbara Strickler dressed up for Sunday, spring 1955. They lived on Lane Street across from Farrell-Cheek Foundry. *Courtesy of Barbara Garrett*

David Sehlmeyer in front of his home at 1536 Pearl St., March 6, 1955. The sign on his basket reads "Drink Sandusky Kist." *Courtesy of Gary R. Mussell*

John C. Bahnsen Sr. worked for the city of Sandusky and supplied work horses for the city. His home and barn were on the 1100 block of Sixth Street. *Courtesy of Merita R. Wright*

Norbert and Marilyn Boose with their children, Judy and Edward, Christmas Day, 1952. They lived in Sandusky in MacArthur Park, an area of temporary housing for returning World War II veterans. *Courtesy of Edward Albert Boose*

David and Diane Sehlmeyer with Santa at the Cookie House in downtown Sandusky, 1955. *Courtesy of Gary R. Mussell*

Mary and Stephen Sartor in front of grandfather Carl Sartor's iris gardens on the corner of Monroe and Camp streets, 1955. *Courtesy of Stephen J. Sartor*

Virginia Grathwol, first woman elected as Erie County Treasurer, 1955. She served in that role for 36 years. *Courtesy of Janis Grathwol Burke*

Joan and Phil Johnson at their home on Dallas Avenue in Columbus Park, Christmas 1958. *Courtesy of Sheila Pfanner*

Jeff and Carole Vaughan on Christmas morning, 1959. They lived at 10 Mill St., Berlin Heights. *Courtesy of Becky Coleman*

Leonard and Cecelia Kromer family at the home of their eldest daughter, Louis and Evelyn Zeller, McCartney Road, Christmas 1959. *Courtesy of Evelyn Zeller*

First communion at the Bahnsen family home, 506 McKelvey St., 1954. Front row, left to right: Pamela, Marsha and Merita Bahnsen. Back row: Ruth Bahnsen, Eliza Bahnsen and Mary Steinhauser. *Courtesy of Merita R. Wright*

Birthday time for Douglas and Louis Zeller Jr., sons of Louis and Evelyn Zeller, 1957. *Courtesy of Evelyn Zeller*

Jean Dix in front of Hotel Rieger, 1955. *Courtesy of Wendell Blevins*

Logan Bickley holding Moreen, Cathy, Gary, Barbara, Deborah, and Ted in their yard on Kelleys Island, circa 1961. *Courtesy of Ted and Barbara Blatt*

Wilma and John Gast, 1523 Camp St., circa 1960. They raised seven children in this home along with John's small but perfect garden and Wilma's beautiful roses. *Courtesy of Brenda Bahnsen*

Wilken family and neighbors saluting the flag, 1961, Bay View. Front row, left to right: Mike, Jeff, Tim, Pat, Julie and Amy Wilken. Mother Joann Wilken is on the back right pointing her finger at Julie to turn around. The others in the back are neighbors. *Courtesy of Brenda Bahnsen*

Jackie Mayer, Miss Ohio 1962 and Miss America 1963. *Courtesy of Jackie Mayer*

Arnold Scheele, an artist from Kelleys Island who taught at Michigan State University. *Courtesy of Sandusky Library NBRC-354*

Charles J. Andres Sr. and Carol M. Andres with their son, Charles J. Andres Jr., at the home of Amelia and John Ontal, 2018 Wilson St., February 1965. *Courtesy of Lara B. Wilken*

William and Norma Bickley family, 1963. Seated, left to right: Pat, Norma, William and Marilyn. Standing: Anita, Laddy, Billy, Jim "Snooky," Brad, Bobby, Herman and Betty. William Victor Bickley was a World War I marine who fought in the Argonne Forest in France. He was a lifetime member of the Sandusky VFW and was the last active World War I veteran in the organization. *Courtesy of Betty Mingus*

Joan Johnson with her daughter, Joy, in Columbus Park, 1962. *Courtesy of Sheila Pfanner*

Buford Blevins with his two-year-old son, Wendell, and dog, Smokey, June 1963. They lived on Rt. 99 in Sandusky. *Courtesy of Wendell Blevins*

FAMILY & FRIENDS

Picnic at East Harbor State Park, circa 1965. Back, left to right: Stephen Gast holding Christopher Gast, Amy Wilken, Julie Wilken and Joann Wilken. Jean Gast is in the back right corner. Front: Marty Gast, Tim Wilken, Pat Wilken, Kathy Gast and Carolyn Gast. *Courtesy of Brenda Bahnsen*

Fun in Grandma's sleigh, 606 Wayne St., 1969. Scott Porterfield and Joanne Speers are in front, Sue Porterfield and Rick Waldock in the middle and Ellen Waldock and Jenny Speers in the back. *Courtesy of Judy Porterfield*

Johnson kids on the first day of school, 1971. From left to right: Philip, Sheila, Joy and younger brother Patrick. *Courtesy of Sheila Pfanner*

Participants of a neighborhood football game on Cement Avenue on the west end of Sandusky, 1970. Front row, left to right: Mark Esposito, Jeff LaCourse, Jerry LaCourse and Brian Lindsley. Back row: Vicky Esposito, Donald LaCourse Jr. and William LaCourse. *Courtesy of Donald LaCourse Jr.*

Ed Wimmer and Evelyn Zeller on board the charter fishing boat the *Wahoo* on Lake Erie near Kelleys Island, circa 1975. *Courtesy of Evelyn Zeller*

Leonard and Cecelia Kromer family, April 1967, at Holy Angels Church. Front row, left to right: Carole Kromer, Cecelia Kromer, Charles Kromer, Sister Mary Mona and Ramona Kromer. Back row: Gilbert Kromer, Evelyn Zeller, Russell Kromer, Dr. Robert Kromer and twins Marjorie Bauer and Kenneth Kromer. *Courtesy of Evelyn Zeller*

VIEWS

The view from here has always been defined by Lake Erie and the Sandusky Bay, and the beauty of it always survived the changing landscape.

Steamers shipped in and out bringing coal and other resources and giving residents a big view of the big ships, and the waterfront was always a destination for a family drive.

But great stone buildings also have grounded communities, from the Erie County Courthouse and the old Sandusky High School (Adams Junior High) downtown to the castles of the Old Soldiers & Sailors Home (Ohio Veterans Home) in Perkins Township.

Freighters at the coal docks at Sandusky, circa 1948. They are making preparations for starting a new season after spending the winter at the docks. *Courtesy of Tom Hartley*

VIEWS

Train at Railroad Street in Sandusky, circa 1940. *Courtesy of Sandusky Library SAPI-572*

Coal docks No. 1 and No. 2 at the foot of King Street, 1940. *Courtesy of Bob and Barb Volz*

The foot of Dutch Lane in the cove off Meigs Street, circa 1941. *Courtesy of Bob and Barb Volz*

Underground Comfort Station in Washington Park during an ice storm, 1942. *Courtesy of Bob and Barb Volz*

Sandusky waterworks on Meigs Street, circa 1940. *Courtesy of Bob and Barb Volz*

Aerial view of the Plum Brook Ordnance Works in Perkins Township, July 1, 1941. *Courtesy of Sandusky Library 80-5088C*

The Blue Hole in Castalia, 1943. *Courtesy of Sandusky Library NBRC-297*

The beginning of construction for the Huron Grain Elevator, 1946.
Courtesy of Sandusky Library NBRC-320

View of the waterfront with Billman Yacht Sales in the foreground.
Courtesy of Wilma Daugherty

Taking down the Opera House, June 1955. *Courtesy of Sandusky Library SAPI-779*

VIEWS

At Battery Park can be seen, beginning at the left, Lay Brothers Fisheries building, a tower for civil defense air watch, and the Battery Park concession building, Feb. 3, 1955. *Courtesy of Sandusky Library SAPK-001*

Slate cut at Barnes curve on Route 2 near Huron, circa 1950.
Courtesy of Sandusky Library NBRC-330

Blue Hole entrance, Castalia, circa 1955. *Courtesy of Bruce Martin*

The beginning of construction for the Huron Grain Elevator, 1946.
Courtesy of Sandusky Library NBRC-320

View of the waterfront with Billman Yacht Sales in the foreground.
Courtesy of Wilma Daugherty

Taking down the Opera House, June 1955. *Courtesy of Sandusky Library SAPI-779*

VIEWS

At Battery Park can be seen, beginning at the left, Lay Brothers Fisheries building, a tower for civil defense air watch, and the Battery Park concession building, Feb. 3, 1955. *Courtesy of Sandusky Library SAPK-001*

Slate cut at Barnes curve on Route 2 near Huron, circa 1950.
Courtesy of Sandusky Library NBRC-330

Blue Hole entrance, Castalia, circa 1955. *Courtesy of Bruce Martin*

Site of the future The Harbor and Radisson Hotel complex development on the east side of Sandusky, 1958. *Courtesy of Tom Root*

Looking toward the foot of Columbus Avenue, 1958. On the right can be seen the last ice house where ice cut from the lake was stored.
Courtesy of Sandusky Library BUSI-536

Buzzing the avenue looking south on Columbus Avenue, 1967. Gray Drug and Jupiter are on either side of the street. *Courtesy of Suzanne Johnson*

Municipal boat harbor under construction at Huron, May 4, 1971.
Courtesy of Tom Root

Breakers Hotel and midway at Cedar Point on a late winter day, March 26, 1972. *Courtesy of Tom Root*

EST. 1975

Pierre's Quickprint is your Digital Print Center. It has been serving the area for over 30 years. The business has grown from it's 1,000 sq. ft. beginning on Washington Row to a 7,000 sq. ft. facility on Cleveland Road.

Pierre's specializes in Digital Printing and Graphic Design. Keeping up with the digital revolution has been a challenge but they have successfully modernized all their equipment to meet the needs of today's digital world. No print shop has been on the cutting edge of technology more then Pierre's.

When you walk into Pierre's, you will find the largest selection of specialty paper in the area. A new addition to their showroom is a large selection of custom designed scrapbook paper of all the area schools.

Pierre's Quickprint...leading the way yesterday......today and tomorrow.

1005 Cleveland Road • Sandusky, Ohio 44870
419.625.4073 • www.pierresquickprint.com

HAMMER-HUBER'S
BIG ON QUALITY & BIG ON SERVICE

Our two locations offer the largest selection of outdoor apparel and equipment in the area.

Established in 1967 in Norwalk, and 1983 in Sandusky. Hammer Huber's stocks clothing and shoes for all, including the big & tall man. We have a large selection of work, hunting-western and casual clothes & shoes. Steel toe shoes for men & women are always in stock.

SANDUSKY, OH
1212 Hull Road & Rt. 250
419-626-0193

NORWALK, OH
210 Milan Rd.
419-668-9417

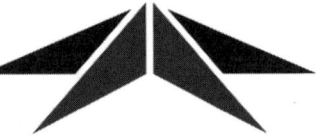

CITIZENSBANK™
Moving You Ahead

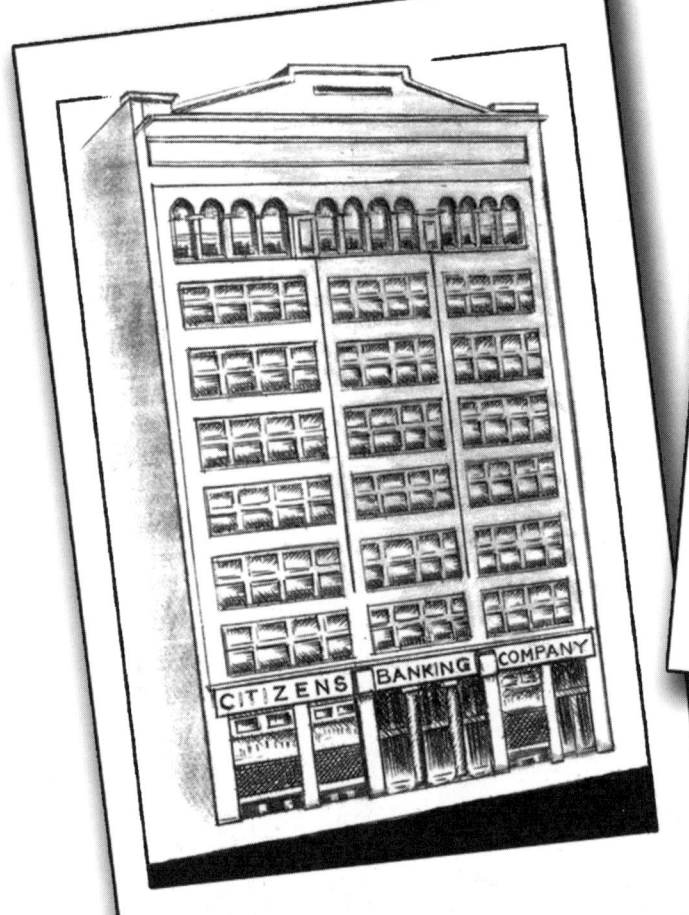

*There for you then...
Here for you now.*

Over 120 Years of Service.